Another Look At
Death, And Resurrection Of The Lord

People Who Met Jesus

Ron Lavin

CSS Publishing Company, Inc., Lima, Ohio

PEOPLE WHO MET JESUS

Copyright © 2006 by
CSS Publishing Company, Inc.
Lima, Ohio

Library of Congress Cataloging-in-Publication Data

Lavin, Ronald J.
  People who met Jesus : another look at the suffering, death, and Resurrection of the Lord / Ron Lavin.
     p. cm.
  Includes bibliographical references.
  ISBN 0-7880-2347-0 (perfect bound : alk. paper)
  1. Bible. N.T. Gospels—Criticism, interpretation, etc. 2. Jesus Christ—Passion—Biblical teaching. 3. Suffering of God—Biblical teaching. 4. Jesus Christ—Biblical teaching. I. Title.

  BS2555.52.L38 2005
  232.96—dc22

                                                              2005022918

For more information about CSS Publishing Company resources, visit our website at www.csspub.com or email us at custserv@csspub.com or call (800) 241-4056.

Cover design by Barb Spencer
ISBN 0-7880-2347-0   PRINTED IN U.S.A.

This book is dedicated to:

Theological mentors and leaders
Martin Luther
George Forell
Pat Keifert
Paul Werger

Special leaders in the churches I served, especially
Glen Knapp
Al Glotfeldty
Duane Johnson
Royce and Cel Schafer
Dick and Mary Ann Clausen
Bob Sohl
Harry and Dodie Anderson
Bud Potter
Rod Anderson
Mel and Caroline Kieschnick

Family
wife, Joyce,
daughters, Dell, Diane, and Mary,
and grandcildren:
David and Peter Pflibsen;
Lydia, Sarah, and Heidi Wilkinson;
and Jim, Steve, and Tom Cousler

Books By Ron Lavin

The *Another Look* Series

I Believe; Help My Unbelief: Another Look At The Apostles' Creed
Stories To Remember: Another Look At The Parables Of Jesus
Abba: Another Look At The Lord's Prayer
Saving Grace: Another Look At The Word And The Sacraments
The Big Ten: Another Look At The Ten Commandments
People Who Met Jesus: Another Look At The Suffering, Death,
    And Resurrection Of The Lord

Other Books In Print

Turning Griping Into Gratitude
Empty Spaces; Empty Places (written with Constance Sorenson)
Way To Grow! (Dynamic Church Growth Through Small Groups)
The Advocate
The Great I AM
Previews Of Coming Attractions

All of these books are available from CSS Publishing Company, Inc., 517 South Main Street, Lima, Ohio 45804. Orders by phone: 800-537-1030.

Previously Published Books

Alone / Together
You Can't Start A Car With A Cross
You Can Grow In A Small Group
Jesus In Stained Glass
Previews Of Coming Attractions
Roots And Wings
Koinonia Groups (A Strategy For Renewal)
The Human Chain For Divine Grace (editor)
Jesus Christ, The Liberator (written with Bill Grimmer, M.D.)
Hey, Mom, Look At Me!

Table Of Contents

A Personal Word
About The *Another Look* Series

People Who Met Jesus (Another Look At the Suffering, Death, And Resurrection Of The Lord) is one of six books in the "Another Look" series. The other five are: *I Believe; Help My Unbelief* (Another Look At The Apostles' Creed), *Stories To Remember* (Another Look At The Parables Of Jesus), *Abba* (Another Look At the Lord's Prayer), *Saving Grace* (Another Look At The Word And Sacraments), and *The Big Ten* (Another Look At The Ten Commandments). All six of these books are intended for individual inspiration and group study. Study questions are provided at the end of the chapters in all the books for study by adult education classes, new members classes, growth groups, koinonia (fellowship) groups, and Bible study groups. Another possibility is to use the first seven chapters for midweek Lenten study or sermons and the last three for post-Easter study or sermons.

People Who Met Jesus focuses on the latter days of Jesus. This focus may help Christians during the Lenten season, but the study of this book should not be limited to Lent. We need to give our attention to the suffering Savior throughout the year.

Focusing on Jesus may bring surprising and salutary results to individuals and churches. When the African Bishop of the fastest growing Lutheran church in the world (in Tanzania) was asked "Why are your churches growing so fast?" he replied, "That's simple. We love Jesus."

Love of the Lord in response to his love for us is what this book is all about. The people in these chapters were magnetically pulled into Jesus' circle of love. Even Pontius Pilate (ch. 6), had a strange attraction to the Lord.

Foreword

by Reuben T. Swanson
Former Secretary of the
Evangelical Lutheran Church in America

In this book, the author imaginatively describes how both well-known and not-so-well-known biblical characters met Jesus. He also gives a vivid account of how he met Jesus as a teenager. These reports of meeting Jesus are given not merely to note the nuances of chance or deliberate encounters with Jesus, but more importantly to record the impact and life-changing experiences that resulted and continue to result from those meetings.

Dr. Ron Lavin, a colleague and friend of many years, has had a distinguished forty-year-plus career as a parish pastor, lecturer, and author. Though retired from the parish ministry, he continues by witness, word, and writing to point to the one who was and is the cause and source of life-changing experiences for those who have met and are meeting Jesus.

Lavin posits that the "little people" who met Jesus are just as important as the well-known biblical characters. He calls these lesser-known people "cameo characters." Ron says, "They show up; then suddenly bow out. Some of us know a little about some of them. Most of us know precious little about most of them. These are the 'little ones'; the seemingly insignificant ones. These are people who pop in and out of the biblical story and are never heard from again. These 'little ones' make cameo appearances and then are gone forever. Or are they?"

Among the cameo characters identified by Lavin are: the father of the epileptic boy, the leper who returned to give thanks, the soldier at the foot of the cross, the widow who gave everything, Bartimaeus, and others. He skillfully describes what might have happened and what words may have been spoken, using his narrative to emphasize how their encounters with Jesus changed their lives and through them, change ours.

9

The cameo characters together with the better-known Bible people (who, as Lavin says, have cathedrals named after them) have one thing in common: They tell the story of Jesus, who in turn, points us to God. Just as they met Jesus, they help us meet him.

This book, one of six titled by Lavin as "The Another Look Series," aims to give another look at the suffering, death, and resurrection of the Lord, by delving into the lives of people who met Jesus. He cites his own life story as a journey of awakening, commitment, and fellowship, one of conversion fomented and shaped by the impact and influence of the experiences of both the known and cameo characters in their meeting Jesus.

Dr. Lavin, in writing of the experiences of those who met Jesus, intended to stimulate reflection and discussion among his readers as they review their personal encounters with the suffering Christ. To assist, he provides questions and suggestions for conversation at appropriate times in the text of the book. Thoughtful readers will have their insights into the significance and meaning of their encounters with the risen Lord sharpened by these questions and suggestions.

People Who Met Jesus: Another Look At The Suffering, Death, And Resurrection Of The Lord is a book that will command the undivided attention of readers who yearn to know more of the significance of their relationships to the risen Lord. By delving into the depth of the words and experiences of biblical characters, well-known and cameo ones, they will come to a greater appreciation of the depth of the life-pervading influence of their relationship to a living Lord.

Introduction

Section One

A Word About Some Of The People You Will Meet

My purpose in writing *People Who Met Jesus* is to tap the human imagination by telling stories of people who met Jesus and had their lives changed by that encounter. Using what I hope is a sanctified imagination, without contradicting any of the known facts, I have tried to "fill in the gaps" in the various Bible stories. In this section, you will meet some of the characters you will encounter on the pages of this book. Many of them are cameo characters.

Some of the stories in this book are about biblical characters whose names are familiar. Many of us know about Peter, Matthew, Thomas, and John. Peter was a friend of Jesus who nevertheless vacillated back and forth between rock-like faith and inappropriate outbursts. Matthew was a tax-collector who became a gospel writer. Thomas was a doubter; John a visionary.

You will also encounter some people in this book who are little known, even among the minority of church members who are well grounded in the scriptures. Some of the characters in *People Who Met Jesus* are not very familiar. The father of the epileptic boy; Bartimaeus, the blind man; the unnamed leper who returned to give thanks; the unnamed soldier at the foot of the cross, and many others who show up on these pages are not well-known Bible characters. They are cameo characters. They show up; then suddenly bow out. Some of us know a little about some of them. Most of us know precious little about most of them.

These are the "little ones," the seemingly insignificant ones. These are people who pop in and out of the biblical story and are never heard from again. These "little ones" make cameo appearances and then are gone forever. Or are they?

Do not assume that these "little people" are any less important than Peter, Matthew, Thomas, and John who appear often in the New Testament story. The "little people" show up in cameos. They appear suddenly. Then they disappear, never to be heard of again. Biblical cameo characters help us understand God as Jesus revealed him.

For example, when the widow in Mark 12:41-44 put everything she had into the temple offering in Jerusalem, Jesus was watching. If you had had a tape recorder there, you would hear more than is reported in writing. If you use your sanctified imagination, you may hear more than the four verses in Mark. Perhaps something like this was going on:

Watch her closely, boys. You have been fighting a lot lately about who is the greatest. Look. Watch. Learn.

You have been asking if you will get a reward for all your hard work for God. You haven't been paying attention to what I have been trying to tell you. Are you looking and listening my friends?

She put all she had in the offering. She doesn't know that I am watching. She isn't seeking praise for her action. She just loves God and wants to express her gratitude for all that he has done for her.

Peter, did you see that? She put everything she has in the offering plate. Do you understand? She has nothing left. Nothing. Where will her next meal come from? How will she pay her rent? She is a widow. She has no husband to support her. She is totally dependent on God. Totally dependent, boys. Do you get it? She, this wise, old, unnamed woman, understands what you cannot get through your thick heads.

She, not the group of you looking for glory and honor; she, the one whose coins seem insignificant; she is putting in everything she has. Quit your bellyaching, your murmuring, and your in-fighting. Watch. Listen. Listen for the small coins to drop. You are seeing and hearing a fortune being turned over to the Lord's work without any warped motives involved.

In chapter 1, you will find the story of an unnamed father of an epileptic boy, one of the "little ones." Listen to him closely. He says something mighty and memorable. In *Mark As Story*, David Rhoads and Donald Michie point out, "... Minor characters in the gospel consistently exemplify the values of the rule of God. (They) make brief cameo appearances and then disappear, yet the role of each is often quite memorable."[1]

Watch for the "little people" who come and go and seem so unimportant. God knows them. God loves them. God watches them. They are the ones who have learned the lesson of the kingdom of God — to love God back for no gain at all. They have been blessed to be a blessing. They know it. They love it. They leave lasting impressions.

A quick entrance. A quick exit. A person who is not named or whose name is soon forgotten may be extremely important. Is he or she an angel, one of God's special messengers with a special message, like the no-name characters who visited our forefather Abraham and his wife, Sarah? Cameo characters can give us the same joy the no-name visitors dropped on Abraham and Sarah. Joy. You who seemingly have no hope, watch and listen for something new, delivered by someone who seems little but who has a big message of joy from God. Abraham's son was named "Laughter" (Isaac) when he was born. If you want joy, look at and listen to "the little ones" like the angelic visitors to Abraham and Sarah. They deliver joy like a fastball right down the middle. If you don't watch for it, it will get by you before you even notice God is on the mound.

Watch for the cameo people in the stories from the Bible. These "little ones" can make a big difference. They point beyond themselves to God. That is what the Bible is all about — focusing attention on God, not self. That is what cameo characters are all about. Look for the people who point, who do not even know that they are pointing. In their self-forgetful behavior, they invite you to participate in the kingdom of God.

Bartimaeus (ch. 2) is another cameo character. Like the father of the epileptic boy, the widow at the temple, and Abraham's visitors, he is a "little one" with a big message. He catches what others miss: the joy, the exalted, the uninhibited, and the unspeakable joy that Jesus gives. He catches what Jesus pitches; then he passes it on. He is a "little one" who makes a quick entrance and exit. Careful, now, we may be close to the kingdom. Listen to blind Bartemaeus and see what "seeing" people may miss.

Watch and listen to the healed leper, another one of the Bible's "little ones" with a big message of joy and gratitude. When it comes to joy and gratitude to God, we are often slow learners. Are we open to being taught by "little ones"? Can't we all learn something about gratitude from the leper?

Mary, the missionary (ch. 10 about John), is another cameo character. She is like Barnabas, the encourager of Paul; and Mary from Bethany, the one who listens. Like Barnabas, Mary the missionary thinks of others before herself. Like Mary of Bethany, she sets right priorities. Like both, Mary, the missionary, darts in and out of our lives, dropping jewels of wisdom and dedication. Mary is a cameo character pointing us to selfless service.

Martha of Bethany, Mary's sister, is also a minor character with a major message. She gets her priorities all mixed up at times, but she is a faithful friend of Jesus. At one point, housework and cooking seem more important than listening to Jesus, but watch her closely when her brother Lazarus dies and Jesus arrives and brings him back to life. Martha knows something we all need to know. She sees something we all need to see.

The unnamed soldier at the foot of the cross has a lasting message for us. He was there watching and listening when Jesus died. Through his eyes we can see the crucifixion and it's meaning in a fresh way. We can take another look at some things we may have overlooked. Look again at the face of Jesus. Look again at his hands and his feet. Listen again to his words. What difference does it make when we really see and hear what is happening at Calvary?

Peter (a major figure in the Bible) is flawed to a fault, sometimes blind in one eye and unable to see out of the other. Stubborn, outspoken, and, at times, judgmental, Peter is nevertheless a man with a mission. After Easter, he is tenacious in that missionary endeavor. Sometimes his personality keeps him from seeing the full picture as the time he told Jesus he should not go to Jerusalem to die, but he is nevertheless a great witness for Christ. Great cathedrals are named for Peter today, but he is a sinner like the rest of us, a sinner and a saint. The point here is that Peter learns to take a backseat to Jesus. He points us toward renouncing self, losing our lives by becoming servants of Jesus Christ, only to find them again in a new way. Matthew, Thomas, and John are great witnesses, too, because after many struggles and false starts, they point beyond themselves to Christ.

All of these people, cameo characters and those who have cathedrals named after them, have one thing in common. They tell the story of Jesus, who in turn points us to God. Bible-based stories reach beyond this life to eternity where God, the *Great I Am*, lives and rules. They give us ways to remember God. They offer us the invitation to participate in the great adventure of trusting God for salvation. They invite us to feel the pulse and the passion of God's mission. They help us see God's reversals. They help us to participate in God's story. These people met Jesus. They help us meet him.

Through these characters, participation in the life of Jesus is there for the taking. Looking at those who met Jesus is like being given a check for a million dollars. You can put it in a drawer somewhere, unsigned or light up a cigar with it, but who would be so foolish? The goal of this book is to invite people to personally endorse the check, to meet Jesus as others have met him and, like them, experience the greatest adventure in life.

Jesus. My life was changed by reading a book about the life of Christ. *The Greatest Story Ever Told* by Fulton Oursler[2] changed my way of thinking. I was an eighteen-year-old unchurched engineering student at the University of Illinois when I picked up this biography of Jesus, along with a book on how to know and tell the weather, and another on Albert Einstein. I read the Einstein book first. Then I read the book on the life of Jesus. I never got to the book on the weather. Still haven't. Jesus is like that. When you meet him, everything changes.

Jesus. I had no high and holy motivation when I read the book on his life. I just sought to be more than a narrow-minded engineer. At cocktail parties and in conversations with friends, I wanted to be able to talk about a variety of subjects, including religion. This was not a high and holy motivation, but Jesus started with me where I was.

Jesus. I, who hadn't been in church ten times in my first eighteen years of life, read about Jesus, but more importantly, he read me for what I was, a self-centered wanderer who didn't know God. My spiritual awakening began by reading a book on the life of Jesus. It was like waking up from a bad dream and discovering a totally new way to think. The first part of conversion is *an awakening*. For me, this *awakening* began with reading about the life of Jesus.

The second part of conversion is *commitment*. My commitment to God came a short time after reading the story about Jesus' life. On Christmas day, 1954, in a Roman Catholic church on the northwest side of Chicago, I was overwhelmed by the Lord. I didn't want to become a Christian. I wasn't thinking about it. I didn't achieve it. It happened to me. Commitment was a reaction to what God did to me.

My father was Jewish; my mother Irish Catholic. The few times I attended church, it was at a Catholic mass. That Christmas day everything changed. I was called into the faith and into the ministry — all at the same time. With major hesitation because of my ignorance of the Bible and the church and my inability to speak in front of even a small group of people, I committed myself to Jesus Christ. I felt I could not do otherwise. There was a hole in my soul only Jesus could fill. "I know this is you," I said to God. "This will never work, but because you are stronger than me I know I must accept what you are doing. When I fail, you'll see I was right."

The third stage of conversion is *Christian fellowship*. For the first time in my life, I started attending worship services regularly. I switched majors at the University of Illinois; then six months later, transferred to Carthage College, in Illinois. At Carthage, I started studying the Bible and theology. Christian teachers and

18

friends helped me make a beginning as a Christian, and helped me interpret what had happened to me.

I will always remember that my turn-around began with reading a book. *People Who Met Jesus* is written with the hope that some wanderer in the wilderness will identify with one or more of the people whose stories are told here. It's possible that a spiritual awakening or re-awakening will follow. In my 45 years of ministry, I have found that people are often awakened or re-awakened to the power of the Lord as they participate in small groups.

People Who Met Jesus may be used for personal inspiration, but I hope it will also be used for group study. Through interaction with Christians, people may discover that some of their ideas about God are illusions.

When someone says, "I don't believe in God," I try to remember to respond, "Tell me about the god you don't believe in. Chances are the god you don't believe in is not the God and Father of our Lord Jesus Christ." Many people need to be freed of illusions they have about God. Small group interaction has helped many people to see God more clearly.

Take another look at the suffering, death, and resurrection of Jesus through the eyes of some people who met him. Discover or rediscover the power of the greatest story ever told. As an old corn flakes commercial says, "Taste it again for the first time."

This book is an attempt to take another look at the life of Jesus. The scriptures are the basis of the ten chapters in *People Who Met Jesus*. What is imaginative is the details left out of the Bible accounts. Nothing has been included that did not seem like a reasonable assumption from the biblical account of the characters who appear here.

When I think of how the material in this book emerged over the years, I am grateful to the countless teachers, pastors, lay leaders of congregations, and friends who have helped free me from some of my illusions about God. There is still so much to discover and rediscover about our God and Father that life is a long journey of *awakening*, *commitment*, and *fellowship*. I hope this book will help you, the reader, in this journey.

The use of bold face italics in the italicized quotations indicates my emphasis.

Section Two

Two Building Blocks
And Seven Story Principles

There are two building blocks in Bible stories: *reversal* and *participation*. For example, Matthew (ch. 9) is going in one direction (self-centeredness and money grabbing), then he meets Jesus and everything changes. He is distraught at the crucifixion. The resurrection reverses everything for Matthew, and for us.

Reversals can also happen to us as we read these Bible stories. The stories in *People Who Met Jesus* invite us to *participation* in the story of Jesus.

What are the principles that build on the foundations of *reversal* and *participation* in *People Who Met Jesus*?

Consider these seven:

- paradox,
- juxtaposition,
- space,
- overhearing,
- suspending the story,
- surprise, and
- invitation.

In this section, we look at the characters in this book as examples of these foundational building blocks and story-building principles. In addition, we consider the parable of the waiting father (Luke 15:1-2, 11-32) as a model for *reversal* and *participation* as well as the seven principles of storytelling.

1. Paradox

The good, faithful, elder son in the parable of the waiting father winds up on the outside of the party (the kingdom of God) while the younger son who left home and squandered his inheritance on riotous living gets into the party. The parable is a paradox about the grace of God. Everyone who will come home to God is welcomed. You don't get in by being good. You get in because God is good. That's the paradox of salvation.

Biblical stories, and characters based on biblical characters, give us a chance to see the often paradoxical nature of biblical truths. Consider the paradox of weakness and strength. Peter shows us both sides of his personality. Is Peter a rock on whose faith we can build or is he flawed by so many faults that we wonder how Jesus could ever have chosen him? Is he so good that churches and cathedrals are named after him or is he a no-good, low-down, dirty traitor? I vote for both. In Bible stories we see both strengths and weaknesses in the characters. Watch for both in *People Who Met Jesus*. Paradox.

Stories in the Bible reveal Jesus as both God and man. That's another paradox. The Bible teaches that God is far away and holy on the one hand; but closer than we can imagine on the other. Paradox. These paradoxes and many more play into the storytelling in *People Who Met Jesus*. So does the paradox that we are both saints and sinners.

God squeezes through an opening in one's personality that we do not even see, and he makes saints out of sinners. Reversal. Invitation to participate. Paradox.

The paradox of belief and unbelief affects all of us. Are we believers or unbelievers? The father of an epileptic boy (ch. 1) says it for all of us: "I believe; help my unbelief." There is the fundamental paradox of belief in tension with unbelief in all of the characters in the Bible, and in us. Martin Luther describes the counterpoint in human personality like this: "We are simultaneously saints and sinners." Paradox.

2. Juxtaposition

Second, juxtaposition is at play in all of the characters in *People Who Met Jesus*. The blind man who was given sight (ch. 2) shows us the juxtaposition of blindness and sight, both physical and spiritual sight. The Roman governor, Pontius Pilate (ch. 6), is a ruler who yelled a lot like it was his to command, but did not have the courage of his convictions to release the innocent man, Jesus. Pilate shows us the juxtaposition of pretended strength and actual impotence. Illusion and reality are in counterpoint here. To pompous Pilate, Jesus says, "You have no power over me." Juxtaposition.

Juxtaposition is at work in a major way in the story of the waiting father. Compare the legalistic, murmuring Pharisees and the resentful elder son on the one hand with the generous and gracious father on the other. Quite a contrast! The father's behavior is incongruous with what we see in life. The incongruity invites us to step outside ourselves, look again at God, and trust his grace for our salvation. In my book, *Stories To Remember* (Another Look At The Parables Of Jesus)[3] there is a more complete explanation of juxtaposition in the parable of the waiting father.

Juxtaposition is one of the ingredients in building a story. Bible stories include incongruity and tension. Good stories work opposites against each other like the counterpoint in the music of J. S. Bach. Stories in this book offer us characters caught in the tension between good and evil. The juxtaposition between God and the devil is at play here. The people who met Jesus help us see evil in the best of us and good in the worst of us.

3. Space

Third, look for space in the stories of the people who met Jesus. The characters in this book do not come out and tell us what to believe and what to do. They don't lecture us on good theology or good morality. These characters and their messages sneak up on us. They just tell us stories, or act out their parts in stories. They provide us with space to come to experience and participate in the great reversals to which we are called.

Consider the parables of Jesus as a pattern for space-giving. Jesus always gave space to his hearers. Unlike so many who rush around and worry so, we find a deliberate majesty in the patience of Jesus. He doesn't force things to happen; neither is he the pawn of someone else making things happen. He just gives space with grace to people he meets and to whom he tells stories. Jesus' stories and actions often hang there in space, giving time to people to get the point, or not, now or later. Given space with grace, many people come to meet Jesus as he really is.

As people heard Jesus' stories, they were often left hanging, wondering what would come next, as in the story of the waiting father (Luke 15:21-32). The younger son experienced the great reversal, but whatever happened to the elder son? Did he stand out there by the barn forever? Is he still standing there? Did he eventually come to the party? We don't know. The Pharisees to whom the story was originally addressed (see Luke 15:1-2) are given space. As far as we know, they never came to the party, called the kingdom of God, but they are given every opportunity to come. Will we stand outside and criticize or will we participate in God's party?

The parable of the waiting father demonstrates space for grace. It also demonstrates another ingredient in Bible stories: overhearing.

4. Overhearing

The fourth principle in Bible stories is overhearing. Overhearing is sometimes better than hearing. Jesus aimed the story of the prodigal son, the elder son, and their waiting father at the Pharisees. They were murmuring against him. "Let me tell you a story," Jesus said. (Actually, he told them three stories, one about a lost sheep, one about a lost coin, and one about a lost son.) Look out, when Jesus tells stories. Be careful. Haven't you done your share of murmuring? Here comes a major invitation to change!

By putting his point about the dangers of murmuring in story form instead of hitting the problem directly, Jesus gave the Pharisees and the apostles a chance to grasp their problem and turn around. By letting people overhear what happens to someone who murmurs, Jesus gives people the best chance to see the dangers of murmuring and reverse their self-defeating behavior. The story of the waiting father ends with the elder son murmuring, missing the invitation to come in to God's party, the precise problem that the Pharisees had in Luke 15:1-2. They were in the position to hear what they were doing by overhearing what the elder son did. They were given a chance to see what happens to those who murmur. Those who murmur against God don't get into the kingdom of God. They stand outside and complain. The Pharisees missed the opportunity to come to the kingdom of God that Jesus repeatedly described in terms of a party.

Today we are in the position to overhear Jesus in the gospels. We are in the balcony watching the action. We overhear what is going on in the story between the characters. Will we get the point? Will we reverse our self-defeating pattern of complaints and come to the party the father is throwing for his children?

By overhearing someone else's story, we have an excellent chance to stop murmuring and come to the banquet called the kingdom of God. By overhearing the words of Jesus, we are more apt to respond positively than if God came at us with a sledgehammer and told us to stop all this self-defeating behavior that will send us to hell. Overhearing is a basic principle in good storytelling. Overhearing is also helpful in working a great reversal in us.

That's one of the reasons why adults like children's sermons. In children's sermons adults are being addressed indirectly. "My favorite part of the worship service is the kid's talk," a parishioner once told me. "I like it because I listen better when you *are not* talking to *me.*"

Sometimes we listen better when we are not the ones addressed. Being addressed directly can be a threat. Being addressed indirectly can be less threatening.

5. Suspending The Story

The fifth principle at work in Bible stories is suspending the story. This principle is at play in Luke 15, the story of the waiting father.

Suspense. Will the father let the son go? Will the boy find happiness in the big city? Will money, wine, women, and song satisfy? Will the money run out? What will the boy do when his friends leave him and his resources dry up? Can he get a job?

Will he survive? Will this Jewish boy from a small town really slop hogs? How low can a boy stoop? Will the farmer give him any food before payday? What will the hungry lad remember when he is starving?

Suspense. Will the younger son come to himself? What will happen on the way home? Will he remember his well-rehearsed speech? Does it matter? Is the father really waiting? Will the father say what almost all of us would say, "I told you so"? Why the ring of authority? Why such an extravagant welcome? Why throw a party? Why doesn't the father give the boy a year or so to prove himself? Why a banquet in his honor? Jesus, what kind of God are you describing who would do such things? Will the elder brother come to the party, too? These are the questions the first people who heard the story must have asked. People who met Jesus were fascinated by the suspense of his stories and actions.

Suspense. The people who first heard the parable of the waiting father were left open-mouthed, hanging on every question. We have heard the story of the prodigal son and the waiting father so often that we might miss the suspense that was there. If we could imagine hearing the story for the first time, the suspense might lure us into the kingdom of God. It's meant to do just that.

In *People Who Met Jesus*, the principle of suspending the story is at work. When the returning leper (ch. 3) meets Jesus, what will he say? What will Jesus say to him? What happened to the other nine lepers who were healed? Why is gratefulness pushed aside in our lives? Put yourself into the story. What questions do you have for the characters? For yourself?

Will Peter (ch. 5) ever get what Jesus offers? Time and again he seems to finally get it only to put "his foot in his mouth" again. Will he ever live up to his name, "The Rock"? Can he ever come back from his denial? Today, in hearing Peter's story and the stories of other Bible characters, we know some of the answers to these questions. What if we could step back into these situations and hear the words for the first time? Wouldn't we see the suspense of unanswered questions from a new perspective? As you read these stories, ask yourself how you would have seen the action and heard the words if you were there in person. Suspense

26

will come through. Reversals (changes) will happen just like they did when people first met Jesus.

Storytelling is demanding in the sense that it urges participation through the lure of suspense. You hang suspended between being in the grandstand and becoming a player on the field. You are given time, not forever, but a God-ordained period of time, to react. Bible stories create suspense in our lives. Sometimes we only get the point later, after hearing a story again and again. Sometimes we come out of the balcony and get into the story much later than the first hearing.

6. Surprise

In Luke 15, we discover an incongruity in the younger son's behavior in the far country. He wasn't raised to act like this. Shouldn't he be punished? When he comes home, we discover the surprise that awaits him. He isn't made a servant. He isn't told, "I told you this would happen." His father throws a party to honor his return. The surprise is so unexpected, the boy is speechless.

The father's behavior surprises us. If we could have been there when Jesus first told the story, the father's behavior would shock us as it must have shocked the apostles. Is this really what God is like? Restoring his children to full status as members of his household if they will only come home? God is filled with surprises. Throwing parties for sinners who return and leaving the responsible son out in the cold because he refuses to come in is the twist we don't anticipate.

We aren't told whether any of the Pharisees got the point of the parable. But we know that they were surprised by what they heard. Shocked. The end of the story is not what they expected.

A parishioner once told me, "I never liked the parable in Luke 15 about the prodigal, the elder son, and their father. It always confused me. I am a firstborn child. I have always been responsible. I have always tried to do the right thing. After hearing this story for what must be the hundreth time, I finally got it. The story isn't about rewards for doing the right thing. It's all about God and his grace that all of us need if we are going to come to the party called the kingdom of God."

27

Twist. Surprise. Reversal. Participation.

Look at Thomas (ch. 10). Thomas was surprised to hear what his friends said about Jesus' resurrection, but he would have none of it unless he saw it for himself. Surprise. Jesus returned to the upper room a week after the first appearance. This time Thomas was there. Surprise. Jesus told Thomas to put his hand in his side. The story is an encouragement to all believers who have doubts and unanswered questions to take them to God in prayer. Thomas said, "My Lord. My God." We can say the same when we are surprised by joy.

7. Invitation

That brings us to the seventh principle in Bible stories: invitation. You are invited to participate in the kingdom of God, not forced to come in. Good stories call for response, not applause from an audience, but response to the invitation to come out of the audience and participate in the great reversals that God wants to work in our lives.

Helmut Thielicke, in his book, *The Waiting Father*, tells the story of his young son who was looking in the mirror one day, only to make this startling discovery: "That's me." Stories like the one we have been examining in Luke 15 invite us to look in the mirror of God's Word and make the discovery: "That's me."

The invitation in Luke 15, and in all the stories in *People Who Met Jesus*, is to come home to God through Jesus Christ by the magnetic power of the Holy Spirit. It is my hope that by looking at the foundation blocks and principles listed here, you, the reader, will not only look for these story dynamics at work in the chapters, but see them at work in your live as well and say about many of the characters in *People Who Met Jesus*, "That's me."

Are there only seven principles in the mix called storytelling? No, I'm sure there are more. If I had written this book a year ago, I probably would have named only five. By next year, I expect that I will have discovered another three or four. But for now, these seven will have to do.

Questions For Your Personal Consideration
And/Or Group Discussion

1. What are the two building blocks of Bible stories mentioned here?
   a.
   b.

2. How do you see these building blocks at work in your life?

3. What are the seven principles mentioned in Section Two of this Introduction?
   a.
   b.
   c.
   d.
   e.
   f.
   g.

4. Can you list any more?

5. How are these principles at work in your life?

Part One

The Suffering
Of Jesus

Taking Up The Cross

He [Jesus] then began to teach them that the Son of Man must suffer many things and be rejected by the elders, chief priests and teachers of the law, and that he must be killed and after three days rise again. He spoke plainly about this, and Peter took him aside and began to rebuke him.

But when Jesus turned and looked at his disciples, he rebuked Peter. "Get behind me, Satan!" he said. "You do not have in mind the things of God, but the things of men."

Then he called the crowd to him along with his disciples and said: "If anyone would come after me, he must deny himself and take up his cross and follow me. For whoever wants to save his life will lose it, but whoever loses his life for me and for the gospel will save it. What good is it for a man to gain the whole world, yet forfeit his soul? Or what can a man give in exchange for his soul? If anyone is ashamed of me and my words in this adulterous and sinful generation, the Son of Man will be ashamed of him when he comes in his Father's glory with the holy angels.

— Mark 8:31-38

Chapter One

Father Of An Epileptic

Mark 9:14-32

It started with an epiphany. It was followed by an argument. It ended with a miracle and a prediction of the cross. It was the hinge on which the story of Jesus swung.

The life of Jesus took a sudden, wonder-filled yet frightening shift when he went to a mountain and was transfigured before the eyes of Peter, James, and John (Mark 9:2-13). The transfiguration was an epiphany or manifestation of the glory that would one day come. But first, suffering must come. Unbelievable suffering. The cross.

As they were coming down the mountain, Jesus gave orders not to tell anyone about the transfiguration until the Son of Man had risen from the dead. Death? No, it couldn't be. Jesus' three special friends, Peter, James, and John, had just seen a heavenly revelation. They had just seen Moses and Elijah on the mountain. Death? No way. Yet, Jesus had said it would happen (Mark 8:31). Now he was affirming the prediction. Resurrection, yes, but not before death.

The three were thinking about this prediction when they descended to the place where the other nine apostles were having an argument. What was the trouble? Why the crowd? Who was that strange boy? Who was that man with a twisted face?

"What are you arguing about?" Jesus asked.

The man with a twisted face explained, "Teacher, I brought you my son, who is possessed by a spirit that has robbed him of speech ... I asked your disciples to drive out the spirit, but they couldn't do it." So that's why his face was twisted. He was frustrated by the apostles. He was also frustrated by the teachers of the law. And, he was angry.

His anger started because of the powerless apostles. The anger compounded because of the argument the teachers of the law had started with the apostles. He wanted help for his son, and these people were debating theology.

The frustrated father must have been thinking something like this: *My son should be running, jumping, playing, and laughing like the other boys. Instead, suffering upon suffering piles up. Something divisive and evil is ruling my boy and me. Divisions, conflict, and confusion. Anger and resentment. I'm about to burst with frustration.*

The man stepped up closer to Jesus and said, "Since you weren't here, I asked your disciples to heal him, but they failed. That's when the argument broke out. Teacher, all I want is help for my boy. He is possessed by an evil spirit. It throws him to the ground in convulsions and causes him to grind his teeth and foam at the mouth."

If we could overhear the father's thoughts, we might hear something like this, *These disciples of yours are as powerless as the others who said they could help. Empty words. Empty promises. We are faced here with something so evil I have almost lost hope. Jesus can you do anything? Can you really help? Just relieve the pain a little. Someone has to help. Look at him there. Have mercy. Is God asleep?*

Jesus looked at the teachers of the law; then at his apostles. He said, "O unbelieving generation. How long shall I endure your lack of belief?" He looked at the man, then at his son. Silence. Suddenly, like one accustomed to command, he said, "Bring the boy to me."

The boy was having a convulsion, writhing on the ground like a crazed animal. Jesus turned to the father: "How long has he been like this?" Jesus looked at him with eyes that seemed to look into the man's soul.

"From childhood. Sometimes he throws himself into a fire or into a river or lake," he sobbed. "If you can do anything, take pity on us and help us," he blurted out.

There was murmuring in the crowd. What would Jesus do? Silence. An awkward silence.

"You said, 'If I can,' " Jesus said. "Everything is possible for him who believes."

The father of the epileptic boy blurted out: "I believe; help my unbelief."

Two things were being said here. First, "I don't understand it all, but I believe as much as I understand, as much as I can." Second, "I need help with what I don't believe because I don't yet understand fully who you are and what you are doing. I want to believe. Help me."

Jesus accepted the staggering faith of the father. Turning to the boy on the ground, he slid into the boy's pain. After a moment, he raised up to his full stature and with a raw, naked power unlike anything the father had ever seen, he said to the spirit who possessed the boy, "Come out. I command you, come out of him and never enter him again."

Silence. Then a violent shaking. A shrieking. A convulsion. Then silence again. The boy just laid there. "He's dead," someone in the crowd whispered. Dead? What kind of healer is this? What do we do now? Bury him? Say a few nice words about him at the funeral?

Jesus looked intensely at the boy. "His eyelids are moving," someone close to the boy said. Gently, Jesus extended his hand and lifted the boy to his feet.

"Here is your son," he said to the startled father.

"Father, I feel funny. I never felt like this before. What happened?" the boy asked.

"Don't be afraid, son. Jesus just healed you." He grasped his son in a vice-like hug and wept unashamedly, not caring who saw him. He turned to thank Jesus for what he had done. He was gone. "Someone tell me. Where did Jesus go? I must talk to him."

"He's gone. He went into that house over there," someone in the crowd said.

Scooping up his son, he ran to the place. He didn't even knock; he just hurried in. Jesus was talking with his apostles. They were asking about why *they* hadn't been able to drive out the evil spirit. The father overheard them talking, looking for an opportunity to thank Jesus. With sadness in his eyes, Jesus said, "This kind comes out only by prayer."

The apostles were baffled. "We pray," one protested softly.

"Not like him," another said. "I watched him pray one day. I've never seen anything like it. There was an intimacy there that defies description."

"That father asked for help with his unbelief," Jesus said. "God always listens when people ask for help. Others should follow that example."

The father was embarrassed and amazed by Jesus' words. The miracle was not just what happened to the boy. The miracle was also what happened to him. A more solid faith in God was forming. Nothing would ever be the same again.

He watched and listened as Jesus said, "Time to leave, men. Let us be going. We must be about my Father's business. There will be conflict and opposition. Suffering and death."

Jesus started to leave. The baffled father had to stop him. He didn't know what was meant by the prediction of suffering and death, but he knew what Jesus had done for his son.

"Words fail me," he began. Floundering for the right thing to say, he blundered, "Thank you."

Jesus smiled at him, without words saying, "I know. Now grow."

That's what he says to all who cry out, "I believe; help my unbelief."

This event was a hinge on which the story of Jesus swung from teachings and miracles to the cross. It started with the transfiguration. It was followed by an argument, a miracle, and a confession. It ended with a prediction of death and resurrection. Jesus set his face toward Jerusalem.

Questions For Your Personal Consideration And/Or Group Discussion

1. Read Mark 9:2-13 and Mark 9:14-29. Do you see any connection between the Transfiguration of Jesus and the healing of the boy?

2. Read Mark 9:30-32. Note Jesus announced his betrayal and death. Do you see any connection between these words and the story of the father who said, "I believe; help my unbelief"?

3. What do you think Jesus' apostles and the teachers of the law were arguing about in Mark 9:14?

4. What causes arguments?

5. What causes religious arguments?

6. Do you agree or disagree with the following statement?

    All believers have some doubts. The question is not, "Do you believe or doubt?" The real question is, "Which of these twins is getting your time and attention?" What gets your attention, gets you.

Chapter Two

A Grateful Samaritan Leper

Luke 17:11-19

Prelude

The Jews of Jesus' day had no dealings with the Samaritans. When Nebuchadnezzar and the conquerors of Babylon sacked Jerusalem in 586 B.C., they deported the Jews to Babylon (today's Iraq). Only the weak and poor who would cause no uprisings were left in Judah. Those who were left wandered into marriages with the pagans of the area. They also wandered into idolatry. The Samaritans lived in a land called Samaria between Judah (the southern kingdom) and Israel (the northern kingdom).

When the Jews returned from Babylonian captivity, they started to rebuild the walls of Jerusalem and the Jewish Temple. They also started to rebuild their long and wonderful tradition of monotheism. One of the implications of rebuilding faith in the one, true God was that the Jews condemned those who had compromised monotheism. The returning Jews and those who followed them hated the Samaritans.

The Outcasts

Hundreds of years later, in Jesus' day, the Jews continued to hate and avoid the Samaritans. Since Samaria was between Judah and Israel (then known as Galilee), the Jews of Jesus' day traveled many extra miles out of the way to avoid Samaria and the outcast

Samaritans. Jesus' attitude and actions toward the Samaritans caused a scandal with his countrymen.

Scandal. Jesus demonstrated the need for a reversal of attitude toward all outcasts and the Samaritans in particular. He shocked his followers by going into Samaria and talking with a Samaritan woman (John 4:1-42). Through that woman, Jesus met and converted many Samaritans. He included them in the invitation to come into the kingdom of God. Reversal.

The scandal of including the hated Samaritans in the kingdom invitation was compounded when Jesus told the parable of the good Samaritan (Luke 10:25-37). Jesus even had the audacity to tell a Jewish lawyer to follow the example of the good Samaritan. There is an invitation to participate in this reversal as we hear the words, "Go and do likewise" (Luke 10:37).

The scandal of including estranged outcasts in the invitation to come to God through faith was further compounded when Jesus met a Samaritan leper and nine Jewish lepers on the border between Galilee and Samaria. We pick up the story in Luke 17:11.

Now on his way to Jerusalem, Jesus traveled along the border between Samaria and Galilee. As he was going into a village, ten men who had leprosy met him. They stood at a distance and called out in a loud voice, "Jesus, Master, have pity on us."

Compassion For Outcasts

Note that Jesus was steadfastly headed toward Jerusalem where he would suffer and die. His mind was fixed on what we call his passion, the indescribable suffering and death necessary to redeem us from the steel grip of sin. Yet, he was moved by the cry for pity from the ten lepers. Jesus was moved with compassion.

Compassion. Coming with passion. That's what set up the possibility of the Samaritan leper being one of the special people who met Jesus.

John V. Taylor, author of *The Go Between God*, says about Jesus:

40

It is his unquestioning availability to all who cross his path and his openness as a man among men that we see what it means for a person to be possessed and driven by the wind of the Spirit.[4]

By the alchemy of his unquestioning availability and supreme awareness, Jesus also introduced us to the Samaritan leper in our story. Without compassion, there would not have been a healing of the ten lepers.

All the healings of Jesus were expressions of his compassion. He passionately slipped into the conditions of the blind, the deaf, and the lame. In a quiet little village on the border of Samaria, Jesus slipped into the condition of ten lepers.

The condition of leprosy meant separation from family and friends, from everyone. The lepers were sent off to caves to be by themselves, to suffer and die alone. The dread skin disease was a deep-seated malady.

The condition of leprosy was an insidious and communicable disease. Scabs. Skin turning white. Raw flesh. Decay. Fingerless hands. Toeless feet. Stench. Loathsome appearance. Pain, a daily companion. Relief only in death.

Lepers were required to wear bells so that people were aware that they were near. When the bells rang, the cry would go up, "Leper. Unclean. Leper. Unclean. Leper." People picked up stones to throw if the lepers came too close. "Depart. We want no part of you."

Leprosy. Utter isolation. Desperate longing. Constant pain. A "living hell."

One day as Jesus was at the border of Samaria, he slipped into all of that. The bells rang. People shouted and scattered. Jesus walked straight toward the bells. He approached the lepers.

Jesus did more than approach the lepers. He slipped into their condition. Unthinkable? Was he crazy?

"Have pity on us," the ten cried out with one voice. Their common tragedy had broken down all racial and national barriers. Nine Jews and one Samaritan — all lepers.

Silence. Suspense. Waiting. It was like time stopped.

What would Jesus do?

41

We Are Watching

We are in the balcony watching the drama unfold. We want to depart, but something is magnetically drawing us into the story. Participation is undesirable, yet unavoidable. There is something here that draws us into the drama. We sense it.

Watch. Listen. Feel.

The ten lepers who cry out for help are like animals — pitiful, suffering animals. Some have gone mad. Some have committed suicide. These ten are like a pack of sick animals.

The pack waits. The crowd waits. The apostles wait. The audience waits. We wait.

We listen. We watch. We feel that there is something in this drama we are supposed to learn. Everything hangs on learning it. What is it?

Jesus walks closer to the pack, close enough to touch the lepers.

"Stay away," someone in the crowd shouts. "Don't go any closer."

Jesus leans forward with hands outstretched, looking at each of the lepers with those canyon-like eyes. He looks at each as if there is only one of them.

"Listen, he's going to say something."

"Go show yourselves to the priests," Jesus says evenly.

"What'd he say?" one leper asks.

"He says he wants us to go to the priests."

"A lot of good that'll do us," one of the ten comments as they start to leave. "The priests will tell us to leave as soon as they hear the bells."

"Jesus. Just another charlatan."

"Maybe he wants us to pray," the Samaritan says.

"Not that again. I'm tired of praying. It does no good. That's what they all say when they can't think of anything else. 'Go pray' or 'We'll pray for you.' I tell you I'm sick and tired of all this talk about prayer!"

"Wait. No. The priests are the health officers. They are the ones who declare people healthy and clean."

"But we aren't ... You aren't ... I'm not...."

"Look at your sores ... Gone...."

"My hands ... clear of sores."

"You are ... I am ... we are ... clean."

"Smell the air. I haven't smelled fresh air in years. Clean. I can't believe it. Is this a dream?"

"It's no dream," the Samaritan shouts. "Jesus has healed us."

"I am clean. So are you. We are all clean. Healed. New. Feel. See. Touch. Smell. Every one of us. Clean."

"I must run home and tell my wife," one man says.

"But don't you want to...." But he was gone.

"I can return to my business."

"Yes, but first shouldn't we...?"

"No time. I must see my children. By now they must be grown."

"Your children. Yes, but Jesus...."

The Samaritan's voice trails off in unanswered questions.

Only two remained. "Let's go back and thank the one who did this," the Samaritan says to his companion.

"Yes, we really should, but I must be going. I have no time to spare. Things to do. People to see. I can't believe it. We are healed. I must go see my farm."

"But what about...?"

"If you go back, be sure to thank what's his name for me."

"His name is Jesus."

"Oh, yeah, Jesus. If you go back, be sure to thank Jesus for me, too."

"Aren't you grateful?" the Samaritan asks in a trembling voice.

The question hangs in the air. The man is trying to think of an answer.

"Of course, but there's no time. There are so many important things to do."

And off he goes.

The Samaritan runs back, sick inside about the others. "Look what God has done," he shouts to everyone he sees. "I was a leper. Now I'm healed. Jesus did this."

There is so much to say and no words big enough to say it. "I was one of the living dead," he shouts. "Now I'm alive."

43

Then he sees Jesus. He runs up to him and chokes on the words. Nothing comes out. He falls at Jesus' feet.

He gets his voice back. "Thank you. Thank you. Thank you," he says through tears of joy.

The crowd re-assembles, watching with wonder as they hear the healed Samaritan. What will Jesus do? What will he say?

There, look. Jesus' lips are moving.

"Were not ten cleansed? Where are the other nine? Has only this one who is a Samaritan returned to give glory to God?"

The question hangs suspended in the air, unanswered.

There is no answer.

There's a look of sadness on Jesus' face.

"Arise," Jesus says, stooping down to help the man up from his prostrate position. "Go on your way. Your faith has saved you."

"Words can't express ..." the Samaritan stammers through his tears. "I'm so grateful ... I'll never forget what you have done for me today. I'm so sorry about the others...."

Jesus smiles. "I know," he says. Then he's on his way again.

One out of ten. Ten percent.

What's that Bible verse?

Enter through the narrow gate. For wide is the gate and broad is the road that leads to destruction, and many enter through it. But small is the gate and narrow the road that leads to life, and only a few find it.
— Matthew 7:13-14

Gratefulness. An attitude of gratitude. A rare quality in Jesus' day. In our day. Gratefulness to God — part of the narrow way that leads to God.

God isn't like a vain woman who needs to be told over and over that she is beautiful or a good cook. God isn't like an insecure man who needs compliments over and over again to assure him that he is okay. No, God isn't like that. He wants us to praise him because he knows we need to do it if we are going to be healthy of mind and soul as well as of body. God knows we need an attitude of gratitude.

44

Come out of the balcony. Come away from just watching and listening what is happening to someone else in the story. Put yourself in the story. Come into the presence of God. Feel the reversal God wants to work in your soul. Doesn't the stark contrast between the nine and the one stir something in your heart? Doesn't the juxtaposition of the ungrateful lepers and the lone Samaritan who opens the narrow gate with an attitude of gratitude draw you into the story?

Isn't this your story and mine? Don't we struggle between the poles of taking God for granted and being truly grateful for what he has done? Can't we sense the massive problem of ungratefulness all around us?

Nine out of ten lepers went on their way and didn't return to thank Jesus for what he did for them. Nine out of ten took God for granted. The vast majority of people in our day also neglect to give thanks to God.

Won't you tell them what they are missing?

Won't you tell them what danger they are in when gratefulness is absent?

Won't you tell them about the wonders of an attitude of gratitude?

If you don't tell them, maybe no one will.

Questions For Your Personal Consideration And/Or Group Discussion

1. Read Leviticus 13:1-46 for a description of symptoms of leprosy. How should people with leprosy be treated?

2. Why do people neglect to give thanks to God for all they receive?

3. What difference does an attitude of gratitude make for our living?

4. What difference does an attitude of gratitude make for our service to others?

5. What difference does an attitude of gratitude make for our giving in time, talents, and treasures for God's work?

6. Being grateful in general is one thing. We see that over and over again at Thanksgiving. Being grateful to God is quite another thing. For what are you grateful to God?

For further information about an attitude of gratitude, see *Turning Griping Into Gratitude* by Ron Lavin, CSS Publishing Co., Lima, Ohio, 2000.

Chapter Three

Bartimaeus

Mark 10:46-52

Jericho was a little town near Jerusalem. Many priests lived there. The priests of this town often gossiped about the matters of the day, including a new itinerant preacher named Jesus. One man was particularly interested in this "talk of the town."

A blind man named Bartimaeus couldn't work, only beg. He had plenty of time to sit and listen to what people said. He is a cameo character in the drama of a larger story called the gospel. What Bartimaeus did seems insignificant, but is really quite important. Bartimaeus listened to what people around him were saying about Jesus. Perhaps he heard things like this from the priests:

"They say he is the best preacher and prophet anyone has ever heard."

"Caiphas, Annas, and the priests in Jerusalem hate him."

"So do the Pharisees and Sadducees."

"Some people claim he wants to do away with the law."

"Just yesterday, someone reported that they had seen him heal a boy possessed by an evil spirit."

"Some say *he* is possessed by an evil spirit and that's why he has such power."

"Others report he claims to be the Messiah."

"He what? Watch him carefully."

One day two tradesmen were talking close to where Bartimaeus sat. "Jesus may be a good man, but his disciples are something

47

else. I was in Capernaum the other day and heard them arguing about who is the greatest in the kingdom of God."

"Yeah, I was there, too. Remember what Jesus did? He said, 'If anyone wants to be first, he must be the very last, and the servant of all.' Then he took a little child, held him up for his followers to see and said, 'Whoever welcomes one of these little children in my name welcomes me; and whoever welcomes me does not only welcome me but the one who sent me.' It was amazing. He believes he was sent here by God."

"Yeah, one day people brought little children to him. He reached out and touched them. His followers were rebuking those who brought them. Jesus said, 'Let the little children come to me, and do not hinder them, for the kingdom of God belongs to such as these. I tell you the truth, anyone who will not receive the kingdom of God like a little child will never enter it.' He loves the children."

The beggar listened more closely. "What kind of man is this?" he wondered out loud. But as always, no one listened to him or answered his questions. He was a nobody, a nothing. People just threw a few loose coins into his basket. Few talked to him or listened to his questions. *He must be a good man if he loves children*, the beggar mused.

One day, two women were talking as they were drawing water from the Jericho well. "Did you hear what happened to the rich young man who approached Jesus the other day?"

"No, what happened?"

"Well, I wasn't there, but my husband was traveling that way and overheard what was said. The rich young man approached Jesus with a question: 'What must I do to inherit eternal life?' Jesus told him to sell everything and give the money to the poor. The man went away very sad."

"And no wonder. Can you imagine selling everything and giving the money to the poor? Ridiculous!"

"Sounds good to me," Bartimaeus chimed in, with a smile.

The sneering women didn't think it was funny. They ignored him and started moving away from the well.

"They say Jesus has predicted his death more than once," one of them said.

Bartimaeus strained to hear what was said. The women had lowered their voices.

"I can see why someone might kill him if he has wild ideas like selling everything and giving all the money to people like that blind, no-account beggar."

Whispers. Bartimaeus heard one of the women whispering: "My husband said Jesus actually claimed to be the Son of David."

"King David?"

"Yeah. It was also reported to my husband that Jesus said, 'The Son of Man will be betrayed to the chief priests and teachers of the law. They will condemn him to death. He will be mocked, spit upon, and killed. Three days later he will rise."

"I don't believe it," the other woman whispered. "He actually called himself the Son of Man? He said the priests would kill him? He claimed he would rise from the dead? If he ever comes this way, we'd better be sure to stay out of his way. He sounds danger-ous. Quiet. The priests are coming this way. Don't let them hear you."

Bartimaeus listened. He heard the priests talking about the title "Son of Man." "That's one of the titles for the Messiah," one of the men of God said in anger. "Now he's gone too far."

The other priest was angry, too. "Jesus is digging himself a grave. You're right. He's gone too far this time."

Bartimaeus was locked in thought about all the stories he had heard when two tentmakers passed by.

"Just the other day, two of his followers and their mother ap-proached Jesus with a request for power."

"What happened?"

"Jesus warned them that his kingdom was not one of power but service. 'I came to serve, not be served,' he said."

Two days later the rabbi and the chief elder of the synagogue were talking nearby. "I heard that at Caesarea, Jesus claimed to be the Son of the living God."

"He didn't! That's blasphemy! He'd better watch himself."

"Yeah, that's what I think. This thing with Jesus is getting out of hand. If he comes to Jerusalem, the high priest will nail him."

"And who could blame him? The high priest won't stand for this kind of talk."

"Not only the high priest, but the Romans."

Just then Zacchaeus, the tax collector, came by. "He'd better not mess with the Romans," he said, trying to enter the conversation. The rabbi and elder ignored him.

Everybody hated Zacchaeus. He collected money far beyond what he turned over to the Romans. He was rich, but had lost his friends in Jericho. He threw a few coins in the basket. "Here, old man. Don't spend it all in one place," he said sarcastically.

Whispers.

"They say he's headed this way."

"He'd better be careful."

"They say he heals the sick and helps the poor."

"That's good, but he says such wild things about the kingdom of God."

"Someone saw him just a short distance away. They say he's set on going to Jerusalem. Jesus is coming this way."

The whispers stopped. The shouting began.

"He's on the outskirts of town."

"He's headed to the well."

"Everyone is gathering around him."

"Listen, you can hear the crowd."

Bartimaeus was sitting near the well begging. It was a bad day. People were not doing their duty and helping the poor. Few stopped. Then someone said, "He's here. Jesus is at the well."

Something was welling up in the poor beggar. He had been thinking about it for a long time. It just came out. "Jesus, Son of David," he cried out, "have mercy on me!"

People tried to hush him up. He just kept pleading, "Have mercy."

"Who said that?" Jesus asked.

"Nobody. Just that blind beggar. Nobody pays attention to him. Ignore him."

Jesus looked directly at the beggar.

"Call him," he said in a voice that was accustomed to command.

A man said to the beggar, "Cheer up! On your feet! He's calling you."

Cheer up? The blind beggar didn't know what cheer was like. Life was a drudgery. Life was irksome, full of asking for help when no one seemed to care. Begging day in and day out was fatiguing: mentally, spiritually, and physically. Cheer up? What is cheer like? What is joy? Some people talk about feeling joy and being cheerful, but the blind beggar had no idea what they meant.

On your feet? How can you walk about when you are blind? How can you get from one place to another without help from someone? Always asking for help. What do you mean, "On your feet?" That'll be the day.

He's calling you? What do you mean by that? Why would anyone want to see Bartimaeus? Why would anyone call him? He usually is the one who calls out for help, for money, or for someone to listen.

No one listens. No one calls out for Bartimaeus. He has no money to give. He has nothing. He is nothing. Nothing. Why would anyone call him?

"Cheer up! On your feet! He's calling you," the man near the beggar repeated.

The crowd cleared a path between the blind man and Jesus. The beggar stood, threw off his cloak, and started to feel his way toward the voice at the well. Some people cursed him. A woman helped him as he walked blindly toward the voice.

"What do you want me to do for you?" the voice asked.

"Rabbi, I want to see."

Silence. Tension. Then the voice spoke.

"Go, your faith has made you well," the voice said.

Just like that.

Slowly, Bartimaeus opened his eyes. He saw people who were like blurry trees. For the first time in his life he saw people. And he saw the voice they called Jesus. He was smiling. His eyes were filled with joy.

51

Then he saw colors. "Red cloaks. Blue sky. Yellow dresses. Green trees," the beggar cried out. The crowd gasped. The beggar started to dance and shout.

"He can see. The blind beggar can actually see," someone shouted. "It's a miracle." Some of the people didn't believe what they saw with their own eyes.

Confusion. Arguments. Accusations. Anger.

"Maybe he wasn't really blind."

"Maybe this is a set up."

"No one can heal the blind."

"No one but...."

"Don't even think it."

"Where did Jesus go?" the beggar shouted. "I've got to thank him."

The crowd turned from the man dancing and singing in the street and looked for Jesus. He was walking steadfastly on the road to Jerusalem.

Bartimaeus followed.

Questions For Your Personal Consideration And/Or Group Discussion

1. Try the spiritual exercise of pairing up with another person in what is called "a faith walk." One person keeps his or her eyes open while holding the arm of the other who keeps his or her eyes shut, as if blind. Walk around this way for five minutes. Then switch roles. What did you learn from this exercise?

2. Read the story of blind Bartimaeus in Mark 10:46-52. What would it have been like to be a blind beggar in Jericho in the time of Jesus?

3. Read the story of Zacchaeus in Luke 19:1-10. Compare this hated tax collector to the head of a drug cartel today. Then ask, "How could a man like that be saved?"

4. What do you think about this anonymous quote?

   Some people do not see. This is called blindness.
   Some people see but do not comprehend. This is called sight.
   Some people see beyond what they behold. This is called vision.

Chapter Four

Martha And Mary

Luke 10:38-42; John 11:1-44; John 12:1-11

Bethany was a very special place for Jesus. His friend Lazarus lived there. So did Lazarus' two sisters — Martha and Mary. Bethany was less than two miles from Jerusalem, so when Jesus traveled to and from Jerusalem, he often stopped at his friends' house for rest and a meal. One such meal would have surprising meaning because it would lift up the central question of the gospel story. The central question, "What's going to happen to this man Jesus?" runs through all three parts of the Bethany story.

What happened in Bethany can be viewed as a three-act story, with paradoxical highs and lows, tensions and troubles, sorrows and joys, friendship and betrayal. These three acts are a harbinger of things to come. They are a preview of coming attractions.

These three acts in the story of Jesus, the two Bethany sisters, and their brother might be titled:

1. A Meal With A Surprising Meaning
2. The Death Of A Loved One With An Unexpected Twist
3. An Intimate Preparation For An Undesirable End

In the three acts in the Bethany story we find juxtaposition between frantic service and quiet space for listening, of life and death, of betrayal and loyalty. In Bethany, we meet people who loved Jesus fervently and some who hated him passionately. In

Bethany, we find suspense and intrigue strangely mixed with an invitation to participate in the larger story of the suffering, death, and resurrection of Jesus. In Bethany, we find the paradoxical tension between light and darkness.

In this Bethany story, there is the *dark* moment of rebuke for a good woman who is apparently just trying to do her job, a *darker* moment of the death of Jesus' good friend, all pointing to the *darkest* moment of all — the apparent end of Jesus' life on the cross. In the Bethany scenarios, we find ourselves being jerked around in the darkness this way and that, wondering what will happen next. Then comes the reversal — the light of God breaking into the dark, the darker, and the darkest moments.

Act One: A Meal With A Surprising Meaning
Luke 10:38-42

Distractions are common to all of us. We get involved in doing good things and easily neglect the "one thing needful." As was her custom, Martha of Bethany was preparing a wonderful meal for a special guest. Martha had opened her home to Jesus before. She was doing it again. She was going about her ministry of hospitality with focused energy. So what's the problem?

We pick up the story in verse 39 of chapter 10 of the Gospel of Luke.

> She [Martha] had a sister called Mary, who sat at the Lord's feet listening to what he said. But Martha was **distracted** by all the preparations that had to be made. She came to him and asked, "Lord, don't you care that my sister has left me to do the work by myself? Tell her to help me!"

Martha was apparently the older sister. Verse 38 says the house where Jesus stopped was Martha's home (not Martha and Mary's house). This is not proof that Martha was the oldest sister, but it is a hint that seems confirmed by the words and actions that follow. You judge if she is the older sister.

Oldest children are often hard workers. Sometimes they become like a third parent as other children are born. Firstborn children are often "over-achievers." All the astronauts in the early American space program were first or only children. Most senior pastors of large churches are firstborn or only children. Firstborn children are often responsible, sometimes even to a fault. Sometimes oldest children are perfectionists who do well at tasks, but easily fall into criticism of those who don't work as hard as they do. There is a turn in the story because of the judgmental attitude reflected in a question by the busy, but bossy, older sister.

The question Martha asks isn't really a question at all. It's a critical statement seeking confirmation from an important person. "Don't you care...?" is an implied criticism of Jesus as well as Mary. Yes, but before we go any further, let's stop and give credit where credit is due.

Martha did the work. Isn't that worth something? Certainly. Martha served the meals with dedication like a German or Scandinavian woman who efficiently oversees the church kitchen in a midwestern church. Everyone says she does an outstanding job. Isn't that important work? Yes, of course. Is there no appreciation for those who tirelessly work behind the scenes cleaning up the church or house, preparing and serving delicious meals? Appreciation, yes. Then, what's the problem?

The problem is not in what's being done, but the distraction of an attitude of resentment that gives rise to critical words accompanying Martha's good work. Like the elder son in the parable of the prodigal (Luke 15), Martha steps outside the inner circle of the higher truths about God with her criticism of her younger sister. Martha's situation is a strange mixture of judgmental words and high work ethic. Unlike the elder son in Jesus' parable of the prodigal who remains an outsider, Martha apparently repents and comes back into the inner circle of Jesus. In acts two and three of the Bethany story we will discover Martha as a dedicated disciple. But first, let's go back to Jesus and Martha in act one.

We pick up the story in verse 41 with Martha's resentment in the form of the question, "Don't you care...?"

"Martha, Martha," the Lord answered, "you are wor-
*ried and upset about many things, **but only one thing***
***is needed**. Mary has chosen what is better, and it will*
not be taken from her."

Resentment and anxious criticism are the presenting problems
here. Jesus is not criticizing Martha's good work. She is doing a
good thing, but is in danger of missing the "one thing needed."
    What is this, "one thing needed"? Listening, not just doing?
Yes, that's part of it. "Being still and knowing God" like Psalm 46
says? Yes, that's part of it, too. Taking time to learn what God is
leading us to do instead of charging ahead and expecting God to
follow us? Yes, I think so. Solitude? Yes. Prayer? Yes. Note that in
the Gospel of Luke, the next thing that happens after the story of
Mary's quiet time with Jesus is that Jesus teaches the disciples
how to pray what we have come to call "The Lord's Prayer" (Luke
11:1-4). Yes, but I believe there is more to this "one thing needed"
than this emphasis on quiet, prayerful time with God.
    Could it be that Jesus is telling Mary what is going to happen
to him in Jerusalem? Could Jesus be sharing what is about to take
place when he is betrayed and murdered like a common criminal?
Could Mary be one of the few friends of Jesus who really listens
to what is about to happen to him when he goes to Jerusalem?
After all, later in act three of our story, we will overhear and observe Mary anointing Jesus for his burial, over the protests of everyone but Jesus himself. Could it be that Mary is the only one
who knows and accepts the open secret of what lies ahead?
    Yes, I believe that's the surprising meaning of this meal. This
is the one necessary thing and hardest thing of all — facing the
central question of the Bethany story. What's going to happen to
this man, Jesus? And the unwanted answer: Jesus is going to Jerusalem to die for our sins. This question and it's answer demand that
we pay attention and avoid all distractions. If we don't pay attention, we might miss the gift of eternal life accomplished by the
death and resurrection of our Lord. Not paying attention to this
one thing needed is the churning and turning dark point in the plot
of act one. But hold on. In act two we will enter a deeper and
darker part of the valley.

Act Two: The Death Of A Loved One
With An Unexpected Twist
John 11:1-44

The plot thickens when the brother of Martha and Mary dies. The plot thickens because the central question, "What's going to happen to Jesus?" emerges again with new vitality in the story of what happens to the dead brother of Martha and Mary.

Act two begins with sad news. Jesus' friend Lazarus has been sick. Now he has died. Time to go see him and mourn with his sisters. That's what compassion means, doesn't it? But verse 6 of chapter 11 of the Gospel of John tells us Jesus did nothing for two days. What's going on here? Doesn't he care? Is he too busy for his friends? Why doesn't he just drop everything and go to Bethany? We aren't told. We are left hanging, wondering with Jesus' disciples, "Why the delay?"

Space. Timing. Waiting. These are all major categories in Bible stories. We are not told why Jesus waited before going to see his friends, only that he waited. Apparently it had something to do with the timing of what he planned to do. Apparently Jesus provided space in order to show grace. Act two starts with a twist — the unexplained waiting. It also ends with a twist — the raising of Lazarus and the repercussions that follow, but we are getting ahead of our story.

In verse 11, Jesus speaks of death as sleep. "Our friend Lazarus has fallen asleep." In many respects, death is like sleep. We lose track of time when we go to sleep. We wake up to a new day after we sleep.

A little boy named Johnny was sick. His mother took him to a doctor. The doctor examined the boy, then took the mother aside and explained that the boy had an incurable disease and that he would soon die. The mother was shaken. How was she going to explain this to her son?

One day as mother and son sat by a window, looking longingly out at the other boys at play, the mother read a story of King Arthur and his knights to her son. In the story, several of the knights die. Suddenly, the boy turned to his mother and asked, "What's it like to die? Does it hurt?"

The mother found some excuse to go to the kitchen. "What can I tell him?" she pleaded in silent prayer. "What can I say? I've got to stop crying and get a hold of myself. I must tell him something, but what?" Then she thought of something.

"Johnny," she said upon returning with some food for her son, "do you remember what it was like when you used to play outside with the boys and you were so tired that when I called you to come in for supper, sometimes you just fell asleep on the couch without even eating?"

"Yeah," said the boy. "I remember."

"And do you remember how your daddy would come and pick you up in his strong arms and move you from the place on the couch to your own bed in your own room?"

"Yeah," he said. "I remember."

"Well," said the mother, "that's what it's like to die. You fall asleep in the wrong place and wake up in the right place because you have a father whose strong arms carry you there. Johnny, that's what it's like to die. Jesus said, 'In my Father's house are many rooms. If it weren't so, would I have told you that I go to prepare a place for you?' "

Johnny died two weeks later, at peace with a firm faith in the heavenly Father.

In some ways, death is like sleep. You fall asleep in the wrong place and wake up to a brand new day in a special place that has been prepared for you.

Jesus did more than speak about death. He headed toward Bethany armed with both the sadness and grief of his loss and a power stirring within his heart and will. Before he went to the tomb of Lazarus, Martha met him and said, "If only you had been here, my brother would not have died" (John 11:21). "If" is the biggest little word in our language.

We pick up the story in verse 23.

> *Jesus said to her [Martha], "Your brother will rise again."*
> *Martha answered, "I know he will rise again in the resurrection at the last day."*
> *Jesus said to her, "I am the resurrection and the life."*

In the Gospel of John, Jesus often uses the name "I am" for himself. For example, he says the following:

- I am the light of the world (John 8:12 and 9:1-5).
- I am the way, the truth, and the life (John 14:6).
- I am the good shepherd (John 10:11).
- I am the door of the sheep (John 10:7).
- I am the bread of life (John 6:35).
- I am the vine (John 15:1).
- Before Abraham was, I am (John 8:58).[5]

Here, in John 11, Jesus adds, "I am the resurrection and the life."

"I AM" is the name God gave to Moses when he sent him to free the Israelites from Egyptian bondage. Moses asked, "What shall I say to the people if they ask me 'Who sent you?' "

"God said to Moses, 'I AM WHO I AM' " (Exodus 3:14a).

Jesus' use of that name for himself reveals his divinity. You can speak of Jesus as a great teacher, but you will not be saying enough. You can call him a wonderful leader and the founder of a religion, but that description is too little. You can describe Jesus as the best man who ever lived, but you only have one piece of the puzzle. Until you say Jesus was both man and God, both human and divine, you have not come to what the Bible and Creed claim.[6] "True God ... and true man...." Luther cries out in the *Small Catechism*. Both. Behold: the paradox of Jesus' nature in the Bible, the Creed, the *Small Catechism* and in act two of our Bethany story.

This saying, "I am the resurrection and the life," is another shocking twist in the drama of act two of the story of the sisters and brother in Bethany. If we could place ourselves there just outside the town near the grave and hear the words for the first time, we would feel how shocking these words sound. Shocking. Yes, but also magnetically attractive and inviting. This is no mere man who calls himself "the resurrection and the life." He reaches out to include us in the community of those who call him God, man, and Lord. High drama.

61

The drama expanded as Jesus moved toward the tomb. Mary was weeping. Jesus wept, too (John 11:35). Then he rose to full stature and said, "Take away the stone" (John 11:39). I love Martha's response in the King James Version: "He stinketh."

Bad smell and all, they took away the stone. Then the incredible power of God was revealed in Jesus. "Lazarus, come out," Jesus shouted with the authority of one accustomed to command (John 11:43).

Lazarus was awakened from death by the authoritative words of his friend and came out with the strips of linen wrapped around his hands, his feet, and his face. "Take off the grave clothes and let him go," Jesus said. That's the twist of light at the end of a story darker by far than the dark aspects of mistaken priorities in act one.

The verses between act two and act three in the Bethany drama in the Gospel of John give us hints of the heart of darkness that we encounter more fully in act three. The title you find in most translations of John 11:45-57 is "The Plot To Kill Jesus." The juxtaposition between Jesus' powerful raising of Lazarus and the determination of some of the religious leaders to arrest and kill him leads to the high drama of act three of the Bethany story.

Act Three: An Intimate Preparation
For An Undesirable End
John 12:1-11

The plot thickens in act three. Once again Martha, the hostess, served a meal six days before Passover. Lazarus was among those present for the dinner. So was Mary.

Suddenly Mary did something no one expected. She threw herself at Jesus' feet. She took out some pure nard, an expensive perfume, and anointed Jesus' feet. Then she wiped his feet with her hair. She was taking Jesus' prediction of his death to heart and acting on his words. She believed what Jesus said about his undesirable end.

The intimacy of the moment could not be missed. As in act one, when Mary was listening at Jesus' feet, she is again at his feet. This time she is doing more than listening. She is preparing Jesus for burial.

Others seeing this act, criticized Mary. Judas Iscariot bellowed, "Why wasn't this perfume sold and the money given to the poor?" Judas, whom the Gospel of John says, "was later to betray him" raises the stakes by asking what appears to be a reasonable question. Yet, he is far from the mark. The Gospel of John hastily adds, "He did not say this because he cared for the poor but because he was a thief ..." (John 12:6). The suspense quickened. Tension filled the room.

"Leave her alone," Jesus answered crisply. "It was intended that she should save this perfume for my day of burial" (John 12:7). Gulp. Quite a rebuke! Wounded Judas recoiled. Then Jesus poured salt on the wound. "You will always have the poor among you, *but you will not always have me*" (John 12:8).

Look at the valley of shadows, with dark predictions by Jesus, dark motives and plans by his enemies, leading to the darkest point of all — Jesus' crucifixion. The high drama of the Bethany scenarios is a preview of what is coming. Then suddenly we observe another dark turn: the chief priests made plans to kill Lazarus, as well as Jesus (John 12:11-12). This dark place in the valley of shadows is uncomfortable to observe. The undesirable end is near.

Yet, because we live on the other side of holy week, as we overhear the sinister plans for death, we know these plans for evil are going to be turned on their heads. The apparent last chapter in the life of Jesus is in reality the next-to-last chapter. There is another plan at work here — the divine plan of salvation.

Those who met Jesus were beginning to face the inevitability of the death of their master. Unready as they were, they not only told about Jesus' forthcoming death, but of the ultimate reversal of death. As we shall see in the next chapter of Jesus' life, death would be only a brief stopover on the way to ultimate victory.

The darkest part of the valley of shadows is just a prelude to the ultimate reversal — the breaking in of glorious resurrection light.

Questions For Your Personal Consideration
And/Or Group Discussion

1. Can you identify the building blocks of reversal and participation in the Bethany scenarios?

2. Can you identify the seven story principles in the three acts of the drama of Jesus, Martha, Mary, Lazarus, and the others who were in Bethany?
   a. Paradox
   b. Juxtaposition
   c. Space
   d. Overhearing
   e. Suspending the story
   f. Surprise
   g. Invitation

3. What do you think about the images of *the dark moment* (act one, *the darker moment* (act two), and *the darkest moment* (act three)?

4. Where are you in the birth order in your family?

5. Do you think there is anything to the suggestion of Martha being the elder daughter?

Part Two

The Death
Of Jesus

Peter Disowns Jesus

Then seizing him [Jesus], they led him away and took him into the house of the high priest. Peter followed at a distance. But when they had kindled a fire in the middle of the courtyard and had sat down together, Peter sat down with them. A servant girl saw him seated there in the firelight. She looked closely at him and said, "This man was with him."

But he denied it. "Woman, I don't know him," he said.

A little later someone else saw him and said, "You also are one of them."

"Man, I am not!" Peter replied.

About an hour later another asserted, "Certainly this fellow was with him for he is a Galilean."

Peter replied, "Man, I don't know what you're talking about!" Just as he was speaking the rooster crowed.

The Lord turned and looked straight at Peter.

Then Peter remembered the word the Lord had spoken to him: "before the rooster crows today, you will disown me three times." And he went outside and wept bitterly. — Luke 22:54-62

Chapter Five

A Friend Named Peter

Luke 22:54-62

Jesus had been arrested in the Garden of Gethsemane. He was tried before the high priest. Peter and John were waiting in the courtyard of the high priest's home. As they sat with others around a fire, Peter was accused three times of being one of Jesus' disciples. Three times he denied it. After the third denial, the rooster crowed.

Peter remembered what Jesus said in the upper room when he instituted Holy Communion, "Before the rooster crows today, you will disown me three times." Peter shuddered as he remembered the words. Then Jesus came out. He turned toward Peter and looked straight at him. It wasn't the first time that Peter had seen that look in Jesus' eyes.

Let's look at six scenes in the life and ministry of Jesus where Peter saw a look that gave him new life. Then we will examine six more scenes in Holy Week where those looks shook Peter to the core.

The Look That Gives Life

The first time Peter saw the look that gives life came when Jesus called him to be a disciple and apostle (John 1:35-42). The big fisherman's life would never be the same. He saw Jesus' *look of invitation.*

The context of the invitation was the ministry of John the Baptist, Jesus' cousin. John called Jesus "the Lamb of God." Two of John's disciples heard the words and saw the man John was pointing out. Then they beheld the baptism of Jesus by John. They were deeply impressed by John's words and more deeply impressed by Jesus' words and actions. They followed Jesus, hoping to learn more about him. "Rabbi," they said, "where are you staying?"

Jesus replied, "Come and you will see." They went with him and spent the day listening to and watching Jesus' every move. One of the two men was Andrew, Simon Peter's brother.

Andrew was sure he had found the answer to the age-old question about God's promised one. He rushed home to tell Simon Peter, who was not only his brother, but his business partner. These brothers were fishermen with their father. "We have found the Messiah," he exclaimed. Then he told Peter what he had seen and heard. "You've got to meet him," he said. "I will take you to meet Jesus." We pick up the story in John 1:42b:

> *Jesus looked at him* and said, "You are Simon son of
> John. You will be called Cephas" [which, when trans-
> lated, is Peter].

Cephas is the Aramaic word for "rock." Aramaic is a dialect of Hebrew, often used by Jesus and other Jews. "Peter" is the translation of rock in Greek.

Was Peter a rock? Hardly that. He was impetuous and vacillating and he knew it. Jesus, in his all-knowing look of invitation, saw something in Peter he didn't see in himself. "Come follow me and I will make you fishers of men," Jesus said to Peter and the other fishermen he called to be his apostles (Mark 1:17).

The second scene in the life of the big fisherman who became a chief apostle is the home of Peter, his wife, and her family in Capernaum, a fishing village by the Sea of Galilee. Here Peter saw Jesus' *look of compassion.*

Jesus had just called out a demon from a man in the Capernaum synagogue showing his authority over evil spirits. He showed his compassion. Compassion means coming with passion, intense love.

Jesus came with passion (intense love) for the suffering man who was possessed by evil spirits dividing him in multitudinous directions. Jesus also came with passion to Peter's mother-in-law who was sick with a fever.

He reached out and touched her hand. Then he helped her up from her sick bed. The fever left her and Peter's mother-in-law began to wait on them (Mark 1:29-31).

The third situation in which Peter saw a look of life-renewal in the eyes of Jesus came in the stories Jesus told. In the parables of Jesus, Peter must have seen the *look of wisdom and insight* in the eyes of the Lord. For example, when Jesus told the parable of the prodigal son, the elder son, and their big-hearted waiting father (Luke 15:11-32), Peter must have thought about how the wise words applied to himself. After all, he too was an elder brother. Like the elder brother in Jesus' story, Peter had tendencies toward a short fuse and quick judgment. He often "shot from the hip" without thinking about the big picture. Like the elder brother in Jesus' parable, Peter was stubborn to a fault. Peter must have seen wisdom and insight in Jesus' eyes when he told that story.

Peter must have also seen the wisdom and insight he lacked when Jesus surprised everyone with the story of the laborers (Matthew 20:1-16). It was Peter who set up the parable by saying, "We have left everything to follow you! What then will there be for us?" (Matthew 19:27). The point of the parable of the laborers who were paid the same wage, in spite of the fact that they worked different hours, is that God is not pleased with those who seek rewards for what they do. Doesn't God, like the owner of the vineyard, have the right to give out rewards as he pleases? "Or are you (Peter) envious because I am generous?" Zap.

Peter, do you get it? This is the wisdom of God that is wiser than the wisdom of people. This is insight into the nature of God's grace. Peter, you and others like you, come kicking and screaming into the kingdom of God precisely because you are thinking that God operates like people by giving rewards for work performed. Instead, we are saved by grace through faith. Once you get the point that you are working *in the Lord's vineyard*, can you ask for anything more? When it comes to "wages" keep your eyes on the Lord, not on your fellow workers. This is a story about the kingdom of God, not labor relations.

Peter must have had to re-examine his values when he heard that story. He must have also had to adjust his way of thinking when Jesus told the parable of the wedding banquet (Matthew 22:1-14). This is the story about the host who invited all kinds of people into the wedding celebration for his son, only to discover that those who had been invited refused to come. In the east, wedding guests agreed in advance to attend the wedding and the banquet, and were told by messengers when the meal was ready, but when the messengers in the parable arrived with the specific time, those invited guests "paid no attention and went off" (Matthew 22:5) and did their own thing. That's called taking God for granted. The host will have none of it. Peter are you listening?

The servants of the host went out to the highways and byways and invited others to come in, but when one of the guests was discovered to be without "a wedding garment," he was thrown out. This missing "wedding garment" is a sign of lack of respect for the host. In other words, the kingdom of God is like a wedding feast where anyone can come as they are, but if they start to take the gracious host for granted "not paying attention" to the standards and ways of the kingdom, they are thrown out. Peter are you paying attention?

Peter, in your stubborn willful ways, is it not possible that you will miss God's will and God's ways? Peter, you and all of your brothers and sisters in the human family, are in danger of taking God for granted. No matter what you have done, you can get into this banquet by grace, but you can't just continue in your willful and sinful ways without any attempt to change. That attitude of "not paying attention" to the gracious host will surely get you into trouble. Eternal life is free, but it isn't cheap. To give you eternal life, Jesus is going to lose his life. You've got to keep your eyes on the Lord who is looking at you, trying to show you the ways of the kingdom, including the way of the cross.

That takes us to the fourth scene in Peter's life when the look in Jesus' eyes invited him to a new way of thinking. Here we discover Jesus' *look of authority.*

In Matthew 14:22-36, we have the story of Jesus walking on water and inviting Peter to do the same. Jesus walked on water because he is the Son of God. Peter boldly asked if he, too, could walk on water. Jesus told him to come. Peter was out there precariously situated on top of the waves until he was distracted by the wind. He looked around. Then he looked down. He began to sink. Jesus had to reach out to him to save him from the stormy sea. "Truly you are the Son of God," Peter and the others said when Jesus calmed the storm. They saw the authority in Jesus' eyes.

We can do wonderful things only when we keep our eyes fixed on the wonderful Savior. We must come under, and stay under, the authority of the Lord. We must look back at the one who is looking at us with authority, or we will sink.

The first creed of Christianity was "Jesus is Lord." Within the context of that confession, God works all kinds of miracles in our lives. "Let us fix your eyes on Jesus, the author and perfecter of our faith ..." Hebrews 12:2 advises. We are called to come under, and stay under, the authority of the Lord.

Thanks Peter. By doing it wrong, you are teaching us to try to do it right. We need a clear focus on the invitation of the Lord to come into his kingdom, and a clear focus on him to stay in the kingdom of God.

Fifth, at Caesarea Philippi, Peter experienced the *look of admonition.* In Mark 8:27-38, we read about the excellent confession Peter made in answer to Jesus' question, "Who do you say I am?"

Peter answered, "You are the Christ."

Then Jesus predicted his death, facing suffering and rejection. Peter took him aside and began to rebuke him for saying this. We pick up the story in verse 33.

> *But when Jesus turned **and looked** at his disciples, he rebuked Peter. "Get behind me, Satan!" he said. "You*

71

do not have in mind the things of God, but the things of men."

That was quite an admonition! Then with something flashing behind his eyes, Jesus told Peter and the others that they, too, would have to deny self and take up their crosses and follow him. "For whoever wants to save his life will lose it, but whoever loses his life for me and for the gospel will save it" (Mark 8:35).

We have a major reversal in this story. Peter's stubborn refusal to see things God's way resulted in a look of rebuke for him and a stunning warning for all the disciples about the way of the cross. *The look of rebuke* is the fifth look in Jesus' eyes Peter observed.

Sixth, we discover with Peter, the *look of transformation* in the transfiguration of the Lord (Mark 9:2-13). Peter, James, and John were invited by Jesus to go up to a high mountain where they were alone. There they all saw a preview of the transformational glory of the Lord as they looked at his radiance.

There appeared before them Elijah and Moses talking to Jesus. They were all frightened. Peter didn't know how to react to all this wonder and splendor, so he said, "Rabbi, it is good for us to be here. Let us put up three shelters — one for you, one for Moses, and one for Elijah" (Mark 9:5). Jesus never even responded verbally to this proposal to build monuments. He just looked at Peter. His eyes said, "You can't capture these moments of transformation and glory, just remember them. Just remember the transfiguration you saw." On the way down from the mountain, Jesus gave orders to Peter and the other two apostles not to tell anyone what they had seen until he came back from the dead.

Through Peter's eyes we have seen Jesus'

- *look of invitation,*
- *look of compassion,*
- *look of wisdom and insight,*
- *look of authority,*
- *look of admonition,* and
- *look of transformation.*

72

Now as we turn the corner and look at what Peter saw in Holy Week, we discover Jesus' look which shook his foundations.

The Look That Shakes Foundations
In Holy Week we discover Jesus'

- *look of tragedy and triumph* on Palm Sunday,
- *look of friendship* for Peter and the other apostles,
- *look of encouragement* in the Lord's Supper,
- *look of disappointment* at Peter's boasting,
- *look of deep sadness* in the Garden of Gethsemane, and
- *look of acceptance and forgiveness* as the rooster crowed.

First, we see the *look of tragedy and triumph* on Jesus' face the day we call Palm Sunday. Jesus entered Jerusalem that final week, sharing a preview of what was coming, both miserable suffering and ultimate power. The Jerusalem entrance started with a borrowed colt, with cloaks and palm branches being thrown in his path, and with shouts of "Blessed is the king who comes in the name of the Lord." That entrance, according to Luke 19:28-44, ended with Jesus weeping over Jerusalem for not knowing its day of visitation.

On Jesus' face, Peter and the others saw the paradox of the coming tragedy and triumph. They didn't know what the look meant, but they saw it.

Second, during their last meal together, Peter and the other apostles saw Jesus' *look of friendship.* John's Gospel records these words of Jesus, "I no longer call you servants, because a servant does not know his master's business. Instead, I have called you friends, for everything I learned from my Father I have made known to you" (John 15:15). That's quite a statement! The apostles, and believers following them, are friends of the Lord. Disciples know his intimate secrets. Disciples know his wise words. Disciples know his love. That love will carry Jesus all the way to the cross. Now, the apostles, and all Christians following them, are called to carry the message of the good news to the world, not out of duty but out of devotion and friendship. "This is to my Father's glory, that you bear much fruit, showing yourselves to be my disciples" (John 15:8). When the apostles first heard these words, they didn't know all that this friendship and bearing fruit meant. Everything was held in a kind of magnificent suspension until after the resurrection.

We don't get the full implications either — not at first. Not until the resurrection personally dawns on us. Then we remember the *look of friendship.*

Third, Peter and the others saw the *look of encouragement* in Jesus' eyes at the Last Supper. Repeating the ritual of Passover, Jesus gave it a mysterious and mystic twist as he broke unleavened bread and said, "This is my body." Repeating the words of freedom from Egypt and passing the wine, he said, "This is the blood of the new covenant."

The apostles didn't grasp the meaning at first. They didn't see the implications of this look of encouragement until after Jesus did what he said he would do — die and then conquer death. Only then, did they see that they were to carry on the mission he gave them and continue the celebration of this Communion meal to gain strength for the journey. The apostles didn't understand the full meaning of the institution of the Holy Sacrament, but hearing these words of encouragement, and receiving Christ in the bread and wine as a foretaste of the Great Banquet in heaven, they would boldly face troubles, trials, and even martyrdom.

After the great encouragement of receiving the Passover meal and the assurance of Jesus' presence in the Lord's Supper, a surprising reversal came out of the blue. Jesus predicted that all his apostles would fall away. We pick up the story in Matthew 26:33.

> Peter replied, "Even if all fall away on account of you, I never will."
> "I tell you the truth," Jesus answered, "this very night, before the rooster crows, you will disown me three times."

We overhear the astounding juxtaposition between Peter's boast and Jesus' prediction of the gory details of betrayal by a friend. We can feel Peter's foundations shaking. In Mark 14:31, we hear that Peter tries to get the last word: "Even if I have to die with you, I will never disown you." That further boast just ups the ante for the ultimate shaking of the foundations later in our story. Peter, look at Jesus' face. What do you see? Disappointment. The fourth look of Jesus Peter received in Holy Week was a *look of great disappointment at the boast.*

Jesus' fifth revealing look is a *look of deep sadness in the Garden of Gethsemane.* Jesus and his apostles had been there before. The apostles sat down and rested. The inner circle of Peter, James, and John joined Jesus in his deep, dark struggle. Jesus said, "My soul is overwhelmed with sorrow to the point of death. Stay here and keep watch with me," Jesus said (Matthew 26:38). Jesus then prayed that if possible the cup of suffering and death be taken away. He added, "Yet not as I will, but as you will." The Gospel of Luke adds that the anguish was such that his sweat was like great drops of blood.

When Jesus returned to his inner circle, he found them sleeping. His face twisted in grief and deep sadness, Jesus asked them, "Could you men not keep watch with me for one hour?" (Matthew 26:40). Going alone to pray a second time, he came back and sought strength from his special friends. Asleep again. Then a third time. Then a return to all the others who were also sleeping. Jesus' sadness of soul just kept compounding as he announced, "Look, the hour is near, and the Son of Man is betrayed into the hands of sinners. Rise, let us go! Here comes my betrayer" (Matthew 26:45-46).

Judas then betrayed the Lord with a kiss.

Now awake and ready for action, Peter took out a sword and struck one of the soldiers of the high priest on the ear. Jesus rebuked him, "Put the sword back in it's place for all who draw the sword will die by the sword" (Matthew 26:52).

The confused Peter and the bewildered apostles watched as they saw the sad look on Jesus' face as he was led away to trial. Then with their foundations shaken, all of his friends deserted him.

Peter and John ran away like the others, but somehow met and decided to follow the soldiers and Jesus to the high priest's house.

There, in the courtyard, Peter was asked not once, but three times, if he was a disciple of Jesus. He denied it every time. Then the rooster crowed. Peter shuddered. Then Peter saw Jesus being led out into the courtyard. He looked like an utterly broken man. Then Jesus looked at Peter. It wasn't a look of condemnation. Peter knew that's what he deserved. It wasn't a look saying, "I told you so." That would have been appropriate.

No, it was a *look of acceptance and forgiveness.*

Questions For Your Personal Consideration And/Or Group Discussion

1. Have you ever had someone believe in you when you didn't believe in yourself?

2. Have you ever had someone look at you like they knew your inner-most thoughts and feelings?

3. Have you ever had a life-renewing experience?

4. Have you ever had your foundations shaken?

5. When you picture Jesus' face in your mind, what do you see in his eyes?

6. As you review Peter's life, in what ways do you think you are like him?

7. Space does not allow for consideration of all of the events in Peter's story. For example, when Jesus washed the apostles'

feet in the upper room, Peter protested, then recanted and said he should be washed all over. What look do you think Peter saw in Jesus' face?

8. What does it feel like to be accepted and forgiven when you don't deserve either?

Chapter Six

Pontius Pilate

"... He [Jesus] suffered under Pontius Pilate ..."
— Article Two, Apostles' Creed

John 18:28—19:16

It was early Friday morning. Jesus had been arrested in the Garden of Gethsemane and tried before the Jewish Sanhedrin all night. Now he was being brought before Pontius Pilate because the chief priests and the Sanhedrin had no power to sentence a man to death. Only the Roman conquerors had that power. The chief priests and their supreme court had determined death was the appropriate punishment for Jesus, the troublemaker. The conspirators who wanted his death, brought their prisoner to Pilate, but there were two problems.

The biggest problem was getting Pilate to agree to the execution. As they approached Pilate's house, intrigue lurked behind the eyes of Annas, the former high priest and the old boss of Jerusalem, and his son-in-law Caiaphas, the current high priest. They both thought about their other problem. How could they avoid going into Pilate's house? After all, Pilate was a Gentile. It was the holy Passover season. If they went into a Gentile's house during Passover these Jewish leaders believed they would defile themselves. Pilate had to come outside to them and their prisoner. They both thought, *How are we going to get him to conduct our business outdoors?*

Pompous Pontius Pilate was infuriated by the unspoken insinuation he was not good enough for the Jewish leaders to enter his house, but he held his temper. He was fearful of crossing these priests, especially during religious celebrations that had the potential of turning into uprisings. He would have to walk a fine line. He would choose his battles carefully. No need to make this foolish Jewish prejudice against Gentiles an issue. Uprisings could cost him his job. He must be careful, but firm. He would show those priests who was ruler and who was ruled on the big question. With a sense of indignant superiority, Pilate went out the door.

He sat on his ivory and bronze throne on an outdoor platform to hear the despised priests and see their so-called criminal. He would be cooperative within limits, but he thought, *No Jewish priests are going to tell me what to do*, as he watched a crowd gathering.

What happened next is the most outlandish expression of injustice in human history. Watch as innocence acknowledged turns to beatings and crucifixion. Watch Pilate as he is trapped in his own traps. Watch for the psychological games being played by rulers and religious leaders as they execute their plans. Watch the reversals in the unfolding of the larger divine plan. Listen to the questions of the Friday in Holy Week that we have since called Good.

There are seven questions raised in this mock trial that reveal the tension between the civil authorities and the religious authorities in Jerusalem. These seven questions draw us into the drama of the plot of the priests, the determination of the governor not to be manipulated, and the faithfulness of the prisoner named Jesus, the protagonist in the divine drama, who seems caught in a vice closing tighter and tighter on him until the very breath is squeezed out of him.

1. "What Charges Are You Bringing Against This Man?"
That's the question Pilate put to Annas and Caiaphas in John 18:29. They responded indignantly, "If he were not a criminal, we would not have brought him to you." The name of this game is "Who's in charge here?"

"You judge him yourself," Pilate responded, dodging the responsibility the priests are trying to foist on him.

"But we have no right to execute anyone," Caiphas said with a cynical smile. "Since you Romans conquered us, you let us judge our own matters, but you took away our right to assign capital punishment." *Gotcha. Your move, Roman.*

So that's your game, the Roman mused. *You want this man dead and you want me to do the dirty work. High stakes game. You don't want this Jesus punished. You want him dead. Not so fast. It's not that easy to use me for your own ends.* Pilate looked straight into the eyes of the priests before him. Then he looked at Jesus.

Jesus. Tried before the Sanhedrin all night. Jesus. Caught in the trap of those whom he somehow threatened. Jesus. A broken man. Yet, Jesus looked back into the eyes of the Roman with pity. Pilate quickly switched his glance back to the priests.

Nervously, Annas said, "We have found Jesus guilty of perverting our nation and forbidding us to give tribute to Caesar." *They say Jesus once said, "Give Caesar what belongs to Caesar and to God what belongs to God," but this dumb Roman doesn't know it. We've got to get to an issue that interests him.*

Picking up on Annas' lead, Caiphas added, "And he says he's Christ the king."

Pilate was watching their shifty eyes. "Take him to my chambers," he said to a guard in a surprise move. Annas and Caiaphas looked worried. "What's this all about?" they whispered to one another. They didn't like this move, but could do nothing about the governor's decision to question Jesus privately.

No Jewish priests are going to tell me what to do, the Roman thought as he walked close to Jesus and spit out the next question with a cynical smile.

2. "Are You King Of The Jews?"

That's the question Pilate put directly to Jesus (John 18:33). He was sure the question put right into Jesus' face at close range would intimidate the prisoner. It had worked before with other prisoners. Power. When you've got it, you use it to get the answers you want.

81

Pilate looked at the pitiful, rag-tag prisoner before him whose head was hanging down. The prisoner's robe was stained with phlegm from those who spat on him in the night-long interrogation. His hair was matted. There were clear signs of blows struck to the head, neck, and hands. Jesus' hands were bound in front of him.

Pitiful prisoner. Obviously a fanatic? Yes. A fool? Probably. A pawn in the hands of jealous religious authorities? Certainly. A ruler? Hardly.

Jesus looked up. Pilate was disturbed by what he saw. There was a look of serenity in Jesus' eyes. Serenity. And the prisoner was smiling.

He knows I will punish him severely at the mere hint of leading the Jews as a ruler. We bridge no potential threats to our rule. He knows I'm in charge. Why is he smiling like one accustomed to winning?

"Well, are you king of the Jews?" anxious, arrogant Pilate repeated.

Jesus, smiling more broadly, answered the question with a question.

3. "Is That Your Own Idea
Or Did Others Talk To You About Me?"

These Jews often answer questions with questions. I hate them. What do you mean quizzing me? Wipe that smile off your face. My idea! Indeed! Why am I suddenly feeling awkward? A rapid fire answer will quiet him.

"Am I a Jew? It was your people and your chief priests who handed you over to me. What is it you have done?" Still smiling with a serene and knowing look in his eyes, Jesus said, "My kingdom is not of this world. If it were, my servants would fight to prevent my arrest by the Jews. But now my kingdom is from another place."

"So, you are a king then!" *Gotcha.*

Jesus replied evenly, "You are right in saying I am a king. In fact, for this reason I was born, and for this I came into the world, to testify to the truth. Everyone on the side of truth listens to me."

4. "What Is Truth?"

Along with Pilate's question about truth, the Roman cast a long look at the man. The question hung there in the air for an awkward minute that seemed like an hour. The two men stared at one another. Pilate flinched, then quickly looked away.

This man is nothing but a harmless philosopher. He's not a political threat to Rome. There's something about him I like. He talks to me man-to-man. Those Jewish priests are not going to trap me in their religious squabbles. What is truth? A silly topic? Let's get on to the practical questions of how I'm going to set him free and yet satisfy the demands of those rascals. Truth?

The powerful politician didn't know that Jesus had previously addressed this question and answered it. "I am the way, the truth, and the life," he had said.

Jesus never answered the governor. The silence grew heavy. Pilate grew impatient. "You don't answer me?"

Jesus was silent. It seemed to Pilate that it was a long time. Then Pilate spoke about his power and the drama took another twist.

5. "Don't You Know That I Have Power To Crucify You As I Have Power To Set You Free?"

Jesus was silent again. Pilate squirmed.

Jesus' silence was followed by this stunning answer: "You have no power against me, except that power given to you from above. Therefore, he that has delivered me to you has the greater sin."

Pilate's eyes gleamed with both appreciation that Jesus knew others were trying to trap him and anxiety about who this man really was and what he would do with him.

"Take him outside!" the commander shouted, kicking a chair on the way out.

"I find no basis for a charge against him," Pilate announced to the priests as he once again sat on his throne on the outside platform.

Stunned, the priests protested, "He's broken our law. He claims to be the Son of God. Blasphemy. He deserves death."

The crowd that had gathered roared their approval of the priestly sentence. Pilate's mind whirled with possibilities. *These priests are clever. They have gathered a crowd. The crowd could turn into a mob. There could be a riot. Yet, how can I pronounce an innocent man guilty? What's my next move?*

"He stirs up the people!" Caiaphas gasped. "Throughout all Judea and Galilee."

6. "Did You Say This Prisoner Came From Galilee?"

Pilate smiled, a twisted smile. A vast sense of relief came over him. Jesus wasn't his problem at all. He was Herod's problem. And even now, Herod, the tetrarch of Galilee, was in Jerusalem. Finally, a way out of this mess.

"Take him to Herod!"

Annas roared with disapproval. The crowd roared with him. But the governor had spoken. The guards grabbed Jesus and marched him to Herod's palace. *You can't out-fox a fox*, Pilate assured himself.

Herod had executed another prophet, John the Baptist, and suffered severe unpopularity because of if. He wasn't about to be caught in Pilate's trap. Yet, he welcomed an opportunity to question the man about whom he had heard so much.

"So you work wonders, do you?" he began.

Jesus was silent.

"Speak to me prophet. Remember what I did to John."

Silence.

"Show me some of your tricks."

No answer.

"Back to Pilate," the ruler bellowed as he belched. "I want none of him. He's a fool."

The palace door banged close as Jesus was led back to Pilate's house and the crowd that howled for blood.

Meanwhile, Pilate had thought of a plan, in case Jesus was brought back to him. He had him beaten to a pulp and then brought out to the platform for all to see. Jesus now wore a crown of thorns placed on his head by the soldiers. "Behold your king!" Pilate shouted. He thought the angle of sympathy would work. It didn't.

"We have no king but Ceasar," the priests shouted back. The crowd joined in, "No king but Caesar. Only Caesar." They repeated the creed ten times.

Pilate raised his hands to silence the crowd. His plan had partially unraveled when the crowd, pumped up by the priests' urgings, continued to howl for Jesus' death. Undaunted, Pilate made his next move.

"It is our custom to release a prisoner during your Passover," he announced. "Here is Barabbas, a rebel and a murderer. Here is Jesus, the one called king of the Jews. You choose. I will release one of them." He was sure he has found a way out of the awkward situation. He was wrong.

"We want Barabbas!" Voices from here and there soon became a demand from the mob. A riot in the making. *No crowd of Jews is going to tell me what to do*, the weak ruler assured himself.

At that very moment, a perplexed Pilate got a note from his wife, Procula. "Have nothing to do with this man. I have suffered much because of him in a dream." *No woman is going to tell me what to do*, a voice in his head cried.

"Barabbas! Barabbas! Barabbas!" the crowd chanted.

"What Shall I Do With Jesus?"

It was a sick plea of a defeated, vacillating governor who lacked the courage of his conviction. The priests and crowd spotted the weakness immediately and went for the kill.

"Crucify him! Crucify him! Crucify him!"

Crucify him for what?

"We want Barabbas. Crucify Jesus. We want Barabbas. Crucify Jesus. Barabbas. Barabbas. Barabbas."

Pilate looked at Jesus who was staring back directly into his eyes. How could he pronounce the death sentence on this man? But it wasn't his fault that it had come to this. *Jesus, don't look at me that way. Don't look at me with pity. It's not my fault.*

"Crucify him! Crucify him! Crucify him!" The voices of the mob rang in his head.

He had no choice. He stilled the crowd. He raised his hands. The crowd grew quiet.

85

"I am innocent of the blood of this just man," Pilate screamed defensively. "His blood is on your heads," he bellowed.

Then Pilate washed his hands in a bowl of water next to his ivory and bronze throne. "Take him away and crucify him." The crowd went wild. The priests smiled. Pilate frowned. The soldiers led Jesus to the street that led to Golgotha, a hill outside Jerusalem where the Romans crucified criminals.

Questions For Your Personal Consideration And/Or Group Discussion

1. What flaws do you see in Pontius Pilate's character?

2. What do you make of the frequent silence of Jesus before Pilate and Herod?

3. What thoughts might Barabbas have had when he was released instead of Jesus?

4. If you were Pilate, how would you answer the question: "If Jesus was innocent and you knew it, why didn't you set him free?"

5. The Bible doesn't tell us what happened to Pontius Pilate after he sought self-interest more than justice for Jesus. History records that Pilate was later fired for being incompetent. Tradition says that he moved to Switzerland in shame. One day he went off to the mountains and never returned, apparently committing suicide. Mount Pilatus, tradition says, was named after him. If you are in a group, discuss what might have contributed to this tragic end.

6. If you are in a group, discuss this statement: No other evil ruler has his name mentioned with derision more than Pontius Pilate. Every Sunday, Christians all over the world confess, "He (Jesus) suffered under Pontius Pilate."

7. Read John 19:19-22. What is the meaning of the sign Pilate had put over Jesus' head on the cross?

Chapter Seven

The Roman Soldier
At The Foot Of The Cross

John 19:23-24; Luke 23:44-49

"I hope this blasted crucifixion doesn't last long," the Roman centurion said to no one in particular as he waited for the criminals and other soldiers on the road that led to the hill called Calvary. The common people called it "Golgotha," the place of the skull.

The Walk To The Skull

It's a lousy, messy, bloody job, the Roman thought, *but someone's got to do it. And they deserve it. Someone's gotta show these Jews they can't break Roman laws and get by with it.* "Move out of the way," he bellowed to the people in the crowd.

Then the criminals came into view. They were carrying their crosses. No greater humiliation could be inflicted on a man than this — carrying his own cross to the place of execution. *That's why we do it this way*, the cynical centurion thought.

Some people in the crowd seemed to feel sorry for the criminals. Others enjoyed the cross-carrying ceremony as if it was a parade. All three criminals looked like they had been severely beaten before they began this long walk of death. "What's that thing that last man has on his head?" a man in the crowd shouted. It looked like the last man was wearing a crown, except it was made of thorns. Blood dripped down his face.

The criminals looked tired, but the first two exchanged jeers with people in the crowd who were throwing words and stones at them. The last man was different. He was strangely quiet, but he was obviously struggling as he carried his cross along the street. Then he fell.

He didn't look like a weakling. He was thin, but seemed to have the wiry strength of a man who worked with his hands for a living. "The whippings must have been too much for him," one of the other soldiers said.

"Let's hope he doesn't die on the way," the centurion said. "Our superiors want him hung of the cross for a long time so people learn their lesson, not to defy Rome." Then at the command of the centurion, the soldiers drafted an onlooker, a pilgrim named Simon from Cyrene, to help carry the last man's cross.

"He looks like a lamb going to the slaughter," a soldier shouted in derision. The soldiers including the centurion laughed. "A lamb going to the slaughter," someone in the crowd whispered.

Two voices were arguing in the centurion's mind. The first voice said, *I wonder what he's done? Don't think about it; just do your job*, the other replied. The argument in his mind was about to become more intense.

Then they arrived at Golgotha. The soldiers stripped the criminals down to their loincloths. They stretched the first criminal on the ground and held him tightly as the centurion drove stakes through his hands and feet into the cross. Shouting. Cursing. Spitting. Pleading. Anger. Violence. Fear. He had seen it all before. Suddenly, the man being nailed to the cross reached up and bit the ear of the centurion. The angry centurion pounded the stakes in the second man with brute force, snarling, "They're all the same. Drop those crosses into the holes. Get on with it. Hold down that third man."

They stretched the near-naked third man on the cross. As stake met flesh on the first hand, there was physical reaction to the pain, but nothing else. He didn't struggle to get free. Someone in the crowd said, "The fool. He could have been great, but he was a fanatic who didn't take advantage of his control over people. He could have been king."

So that's his crime. He tried to be king. We'll have none of that, a voice within the centurion concluded. *But why is he so calm?* a second voice wondered as the Roman raised the mallet a second time.

As mallet struck the stake into the second hand, the centurion heard a woman weep, "What a pity. Jesus healed so many of their sicknesses. He even brought Lazarus back from the dead."

So, he pretends to be a faith healer with power to bring people back from death. We'll see how much power he has.

Once again, there was a physical reaction to the pain, but that's all. No cursing. No reviling. The centurion looked into the unexpectedly serene eyes of the man they called Jesus who looked back with pity. The centurion looked away.

What's wrong with you? Don't look at me that way. Who are you?

A man wept, "I saw him with the little children. There must not be a God at all if this can happen to such a good man."

Men shouldn't cry!

Then as he nailed the feet of Jesus to the cross, the centurion heard a woman cry, "Jesus, I nursed you at my breast. What of the promise of the angel? Jesus, I love you." It was his mother. Through the tears, she too looked with pity at the centurion who quickly glanced away.

What's the matter with these people?

The Roman's eye caught the sign above the man's head. It was written in three languages — Latin, Greek, and Aramaic: "Jesus of Nazareth, the king of the Jews." As if reading his mind, the high priest, Caiaphas, who stood close by, snarled, "That should read 'He falsely claims to be king of the Jews.' "

"Raise him up," the Roman shouted. "There. Drop the cross into the hole."

Thud. The crowd grew strangely quiet as the sky turned an ugly gray.

Now king, we'll see how self-controlled you can be.

Just then Jesus' lips began to move. He was going to say something.

The Words From The Cross

"Now we'll hear the cursing of a man being crucified," one of the soldiers said cynically. "At last he can't stand it. He's no different than the rest. These Galileans are tough. They don't feel things like normal people, but at last it's got the better of him."

"Father," Jesus prayed, "forgive them for they don't know what they are doing."

"What's that?"

"What'd he say?"

"He asked for forgiveness for the soldiers," someone whispered.

"How could he do that?"

A dumb silence fell over the crowd. If the sun had risen at that moment, it would have made a noise. The thief on the right and the centurion both had looks of unbelief on their faces.

A Pharisee broke the silence by whispering to his companion, "See? He doesn't share our hatred for the Romans. He prays for forgiveness for our enemies. It's good that these Romans are killing him. He's trying to destroy our religion."

These words worked like a chain reaction on the people in the crowd. Silence broken, whispers soon turned to loud talking, then to shouting. "Come down from the cross if you can, Miracle Man," someone yelled. "He saved others, but he can't save himself," another shouted. The thief on the left joined the cries.

The soldiers got into the spirit of things. They, too, shouted at Jesus. Then they got down on their knees on the ground and started to divide the clothes of the three criminals. One robe was left. It belonged to the man who was stirring up all these comments. They threw dice for it. They rolled once for the centurion, who was still standing, staring down with vacant eyes. "You win," one of the soldiers cried out. The centurion didn't hear. He was now looking up at the three men on the crosses. One of the soldiers handed him the robe. "You won Jesus' robe," he said.

"If you are the Christ, save yourself and us," the thief on the left shouted.

The thief on the right replied evenly, "Enough. We are guilty. He's innocent." Turning to the man in the middle, he said, "Lord, remember me when you come into your kingdom."

The one they called Jesus replied, "Verily I say to you, today you shall be with me in paradise."

The Roman watched and wondered. *Paradise? Is that where you're going?*

The long hours of suffering continued. It seemed to the centurion that hope itself was dying. *Who are you crucified one?* he asked in his mind.

He watched the man in the middle more closely. Crucifixion is slow strangulation. The crucified one in the middle pushed up on his feet because of the pain in his hands and arms. Then he shifted the pain to his feet and legs because the pain in the hands, arms, and back was unbearable. Slowly he suffocated. *Who are you crucified one?* the soldier thought again. *You're on your way to paradise?*

It looked like anything but paradise as the one called Jesus struggled with bony death. His cheeks hollowed. His skin was dry. He made convulsive efforts to breathe. The bloody hours of pain passed slowly by. It began to rain.

The woman who appeared to be Jesus' mother and a young man she called John approached the cross in the middle. The soldier with the robe draped over his arm strained to hear the words.

"Behold your son."

"Behold your mother."

How could someone who was being crucified show such care and concern for others? Darkness moved in, though it was only noon. The sky turned an ugly black.

Most of the spectators began to leave. Some lingered long enough to hear more from the one they called Jesus. The centurion was looking down at the wet robe in his hands, thinking about what he had heard. Out of nowhere, a horrible cry poured out of the mouth of Jesus. *"Eloi, Eloi, lama sabachthani?"* Jesus cried out.

"He's calling for Elijah to help him," someone in the crowd cried out.

"No," said a man near the centurion. "He spoke Aramaic. He said, 'My God, my God, why have you forsaken me?' " The words struck terror in the hearts of Jesus' followers.

"Even God has forsaken him," a woman cried.

Lightning ripped across the sick, angry heavens. The earth shook. The centurion fell to the ground. "What? What was that?" he exclaimed. Nobody answered.

Standing up, the centurion looked at the face of Jesus. *Who are you that even the heavens cry out in agony and the earth shakes?* No answers came.

Time passed slowly. Something was stirring in the heart of the hardened centurion. The words Jesus had spoken, the way he was dying, the look on his face — all touched the man as nothing had ever touched him. "Why did he ask for forgiveness for all of us?" the centurion asked one of his soldiers.

"How would I know?" came the weak answer.

"I thirst," Jesus said.

One of the soldiers gave him some vinegar on a sponge.

What did he mean when he said I didn't know what I was doing? Jesus, who are you to say such things?

Then like one accustomed to command, Jesus said, "It is finished!" *What is finished? Your life? Did you mean something more?*

As if hearing the thoughts of the centurion, Jesus' mother said, "He finished what he came to do." She was crying uncontrollably.

"Father," Jesus said, "into your hands I commit my spirit."

The centurion at the foot of the cross looked agitated. Suddenly, looking straight up at the face of Jesus, he said, "Surely this was the Son of God."

"He must be drunk," one of the other soldiers whispered to a friend as they watched the centurion reverently kneeling at the foot of the cross.

Questions For Your Personal Consideration
And/Or Group Discussion

1. Read John 19:23-24. What significance do you see in the fulfillment of the Old Testament prophecy (Psalm 22:18) about
   Jesus' clothing?

2. Read Luke 23:44-49. In this story, what do you make of:
   a. The absence of sunshine?
   b. Jesus' last words?
   c. The centurion's statement?
   d. The people beating their chests?
   e. The women watching at a distance?

3. Crucifixion is a slow crushing of the lungs. What significance
   do you see in Jesus dying as a criminal by crucifixion?

4. The seven "words" (sentences) of Jesus from the cross have
   been seen as having great meaning. What meaning do you see
   in them as you read them in this chapter?
   a.
   b.
   c.
   d.
   e.
   f.
   g.

Part Three

The Resurrection Of Jesus

... If Christ has not been raised, your faith is futile; you are still in your sins. Then those also who have fallen asleep in Christ are lost ... But Christ has indeed been raised from the dead, the firstfruits of those who have fallen asleep. — St. Paul, the apostle
1 Corinthians 15:17-20

It finally dawned on me. For us Christians, the resurrection of Jesus is everything. It isn't one thing among many things; not even the most important of many things. It is the only thing. Without it, everything falls apart. With it, everything in my life falls into place.
— A new Christian

Chapter Eight

Matthew, The Record-keeping Evangelist

Matthew 27:32—28:15

"It finally dawned on me," the actor who was playing Matthew said. "Jesus said it was going to happen, but none of us really believed it. How could we? No one had ever done this before. No one will ever do it again. He was dead, stone-cold dead. Now he is alive, never to die again. We saw the ultimate reversal. With our own eyes, we saw it."

The actor who played Matthew was Matt Johnson. He really wasn't an actor at all. He was a certified public accountant who worked for the Internal Revenue Department. Pastor Joe Anderson had asked him in early February if he would be willing to make a presentation on Matthew at the midweek Lenten service. The pastor had added encouragement to the invitation. "Thank you for asking," Matt had replied, "but that is during tax time. I'm so busy in that time frame, I hardly have time for anything else."

"That's why I asked you so early," Pastor Joe replied. "Years ago, when you were one of my best confirmation students, I saw that God had given you special spiritual gifts for his work. I still see those gifts in you. Using God's gifts brings fulfillment. Think about it. Pray about it. Let me know your answer by the weekend if you can. That way, if you say, 'No,' I can get someone else to do it."

"Mary, Pastor Joe asked me to do a presentation on Saint Matthew in one of the Lenten dramas this year," Matt told his wife. "I just don't see how I can do it. It's tax time!"

"Remember what your mother always says," she replied. "You can make time for what you believe in. Besides, you are a big ham. You could do a good job." She smiled.

After worship that next Sunday, Matt told Pastor Joe, "I'm going to accept your challenge to play Matthew. I have two reasons: 1) My mother named me after the apostle, and 2) like him, I am a tax collector." Matt smiled. The pastor smiled back and said, "I've been praying that you would say 'Yes.' "

Matt started on his research right away. He read the Gospel of Matthew through three times. He went to the church library and read the article about Matthew in the *Westminster Bible Dictionary*. He studied commentaries on Matthew's Gospel. He asked the pastor for other research materials and got several that were helpful. He divided his research into three parts which he called:

1. The Foundation-shaking Call
2. The Apostles' Foundations Shaken In Holy Week
3. The Resurrection That Shook The World's Foundations

A summary of what Matt said at the Lenten service is below.

Part One: The Foundation-shaking Call
Matthew 9:9-12; Mark 2:13-17; Luke 5:27-32

Matthew was a tax collector for the Romans who had conquered the Jews and ruled them with an iron fist. That meant Matthew was a traitor to his own people. It also meant that Matthew became rich. Tax collectors got commissions for what they did, but Matthew, like most of them, overcharged by extricating as much money from people as he could get. Like other cheating tax-collectors, Matthew was hated by the Jews. Then one day, as he sat at his tax booth in Capernaum everything changed.

Capernaum was a town on the northwest shore of the Sea of Galilee. Matthew lived and worked there. Jesus came to Capernaum one day and stopped at the tax booth from which Matthew ran his business. The Bible tells us only that Matthew heard Jesus say, "Follow me." Two words. There's a lot of space left for the reader of scripture to use his or her imagination. What had Matthew heard about Jesus before this time? What did that look in Jesus' eyes mean? What about the shock of being invited to leave his lucrative business, his family, security, and home? Matthew's mind must have been filled with unanswered questions about what it would mean to follow Jesus.

There is a shaking of Matthew's foundations in these two little words! We feel suspense as we watch Matthew obey the call. The tax collector became an apostle. The incongruity of these two positions is paradox number one in Matthew's call.

A second paradox in Matthew's call came on the heels of the foundation-shaking call. Jesus walked to Matthew's house with Matthew following, trying to ask a question. "Wh ... Wh ... Where are you going?" Matthew must have stammered.

"To your house to eat. Invite your friends."

It was a big house, big enough for many people in town to come. It was a house bought with the dirty money of a cheat and traitor. A few righteous folks were sprinkled into the crowd of traitors, liars, cheats, robbers, tax-collectors, and prostitutes like a little salt sprinkled on the garbage in a dump. In our time, we can only compare Jesus going to a party at Matthew's house with Matthew's friends to his going to a party at the home of the head of a drug cartel. Shocking! Scandalous! A violent act flying in the face on society's values! Who does this Jesus think he is?

That's what the salty Pharisees said to Jesus' disciples. Their comments about unrighteous sinners set up the third shocking incongruity in the drama of the call of Matthew and other sinners to follow him.

The third paradox in the story of Matthew's call came as Jesus overheard the criticism of sinners and faced it down with a boldness and authority that "knocked the socks off" his critics. Some of the sinners were cowering in the shadows to avoid the self-righteous eyes of the Pharisees, but Jesus looked right into their judgmental eyes and said with the authority of one accustomed to command, "It is not the healthy who need a doctor, but the sick ... I have come not to call the righteous, but sinners."

If you had been there, you would have been able to hear a pin drop. What would they say? What would they do? According to the biblical account, those who thought of themselves as righteous and superior in the practice of religion said nothing.

In Matthew's Gospel we find one reversal after another, shock after shock, surprises within surprises, one paradox after another. People who were nobodies, the scum of society, were offered healthy and whole minds and spirits through forgiveness. Jesus did this kind of thing again and again.

Matthew, the record-keeping evangelist, saw and reported these reversals and surprises in the words and actions of Jesus. Matthew reports stunning reversals and amazing surprises — unexpected healings, compassionate actions to the needy, words of encouragement to the down-and-out, words of challenge to the self-righteous, and serious conflicts with those who were judgmental. Matthew reports the foundation-shaking words and actions of Jesus for good. Then came Holy Week when everything good was turned upside down. Evil seemingly triumphed. The devil appeared to have the last reversal. It seemed like the reversals for good were themselves reversed and all hope was lost. Jesus was crucified on a hill called Calvary.

Part Two: The Apostles' Foundations Shaken In Holy Week

Chapters 6 and 27 of Matthew's Gospel record the story of what appeared to be the final chapter in Jesus' life. The beginning of the final chapter of Jesus' life was when the chief priests and elders assembled in a plot to arrest and kill the Lord.

After we overhear Jesus' prediction of his death and the plot of the religious officials to kill him, we watch Mary, the sister of Lazarus, pouring oil on Jesus' head causing confused objections from Judas and others about the waste of the precious oil. Jesus surprised the critics by affirming the woman's gesture as a preparation for his burial. A heavy gloom must have filled the room. Evil moved in like a fog.

The next evil reversal came as the shadowy Passover plot of the religious rulers was set up by the betrayal of a friend. As Jesus spent his last Passover with his followers. He announced, "One of you will betray me."

Confusion reigned as that statement sunk in and each apostle said, "Surely not I, Lord?" Then Judas asked, "Surely not I, Rabbi?" "Yes," Jesus replied sadly, "it is you." While the others were lost in confused conversation, Judas slowly walked to the door, looked back, and left. Shortly thereafter, Judas betrayed Jesus into the hands of the high priest and the other religious authorities.

In the upper room, the confusion about betrayal compounded as Jesus spoke these mysterious words: "Take and eat; this is my body." A little later taking up the cup of Passover wine Jesus said, "Drink from it all of you. This is my blood of the covenant, which is poured out for many for the forgiveness of sins." Dumbfounded, the apostles passed the consecrated unleavened bread and Passover wine to one another.

Then came a stunning announcement: "This very night you will all fall away on account of me." Shaken to the core, all who heard it, denied the truth of it. They turned to one another in confusion. Peter looked directly at Jesus.

"Even if all fall away on account of you, I never will," he boldly claimed.

Jesus looked at Peter. "This very night, before the rooster crows, you will disown me three times." What's going on here? Everything is falling apart.

"Never, even if I have to die with you, I will never disown you," the big fisherman asserted. A shadowy cloud of deep sadness hung over the group as the others said the same.

They walked from the upper room through the Kidron Valley to the Mount of Olives and the Garden of Gethsemane. There, Jesus took Peter, James, and John, his inner circle, with him deeper into the Garden where he prayed, "My Father, if it is possible, may this cup be taken from me. Yet not as I will, but as you will."

When he emerged to where the apostles were sleeping in weariness from the confusion of the night, Jesus declared, "The hour is near, and the Son of Man is betrayed into the hands of sinners. Here comes the betrayer!" The words hung in the air like a fog.

Judas arrived with temple soldiers armed with clubs and swords. "Greetings, Rabbi!" he said. Then he kissed Jesus.

"Friend, do what you came for."

The soldiers grabbed Jesus. Peter quickly took out his sword. "Put your sword back," Jesus told him, "for all who live by the sword, will die by the sword." New lows were reached as Jesus' friends, including Matthew, deserted him and fled.

At the Sanhedrin, the Jewish supreme court, Jesus was tried in the middle of the night before the high priest and the elders. After many questions and long silences, the impatient high priest said, "I charge you under oath by the living God: Tell us if you are the Christ, the Son of God."

"Yes, it is as you say," Jesus said raising his head. "But I say to all of you: In the future you will see the Son of Man sitting at the right hand of the Mighty One and coming on the clouds of heaven."

Matt Johnson paused dramatically as he quoted Jesus' words before the Sanhedrin. He let the words sink in, realizing that Jesus had sealed his death sentence by his claim. "Nothing would stop the Jewish leaders from seeing to Jesus' death," he added as a tear dripped onto his notes. "Some spit on Jesus," he said. "Others struck him with their fists or slapped him, saying, 'Prophesy to us, Christ. Who hit you?' Then, as predicted, Peter who was in the courtyard denied Jesus three times." Matt found it hard to go on. "The rooster crowed," Matt said, trying to avert the eyes of the church members by looking back at his notes.

Matthew reports that Judas, seized with remorse, threw the thirty pieces of silver he had been paid at the feet of the chief priest. He departed and hanged himself.

Since the Jewish leaders could not issue the death penalty, they took Jesus to the palace of Governor Pontius Pilate. Pilate asked Jesus many questions, but most went unanswered. The silence was deafening. Then the Roman had an idea. Trying to wiggle out of the responsibility the temple leaders were trying to place on him, Pilate made a sly proposal to the crowd.

"Do you want me to release Barabbas or Jesus?" he shouted, confident in the answer that would surely come. Barabbas was a dangerous revolutionary and a killer.

"Barabbas," the crowd shouted back to the surprise of the governor.

As Pilate pondered his predicament, a note was handed to him. It was from his wife. "Don't have anything to do with that innocent man, for I have suffered a great deal today in a dream because of him," the note said. *Woman, leave me alone*, he thought, *Who's on trial here, Jesus or me?*

Matthew reports that Pilate asked the crowd, "What shall I do, then, with Jesus who is called Christ?"

The crowd responded as with one voice, "Crucify him!"

"Why?" Pilate shouted back.

No reasons were given. Just loud cries. "Crucify him! Crucify him! Crucify him!"

Jesus was flogged by the Roman soldiers. Then he was led away to be crucified at the hill outside of Jerusalem called Calvary. At the cross, Jesus was mocked. Matthew reports that the people in the crowd shouted, "He saved others, but he can't save himself! He's the king of Israel! Let him come down now from the cross, and we will believe in him. He trusts in God. Let God rescue him now if he wants him, for he said, 'I am the Son of God.' "

Matthew says that darkness covered the place from the sixth to the ninth hour. Then Jesus cried out, *"Eloi, Eloi, lama sabachthani?"* — which means "My God, my God, why have you forsaken me?"

As evening fell, Joseph of Arimathea, a disciple of Jesus, asked Pilate if the body could be placed in the tomb he had bought for his own burial. Joseph and some other disciples took the body down from the cross, carried it to the tomb, wrapped it in linens, placed it in the grave, and rolled a huge stone in front of the grave.

At the request of the high priest and the Pharisees, a guard was placed in front of the tomb. The guards sealed the tomb. Foolish guards. When God decides to do something, do you think armed guards can keep it from happening?

Part Three: The Resurrection
That Shook The World's Foundations

Matt Johnson closed the pulpit Bible and put his notes in his pocket as he spoke his closing words. "We all know what happened next," he said. "Matthew and the other gospel writers tell us that Jesus came back to life. He made a brief stopover in the grave on the way to freedom."

Matt looked out at his friends in the congregation. They were wrapped in avid attention as he told them the story of Matthew. Mary, Matt's wife, had a glint in her eyes as he spoke. He went on with his presentation.

"In Matthew 28:1-10 the tax collector turned evangelist tells us about Mary Magdalene and 'the other Mary' feeling an earthquake and seeing an angel. These earth-shaking experiences were followed by the words of the angel: '... He is not here; he has risen, just as he said.' The women hurried away from the empty tomb on their way to tell Jesus' disciples what they had seen and heard. Suddenly, from out of nowhere, the Lord stopped them and said, 'Greetings. Do not be afraid. Go and tell my brothers to go to Galilee; there you will see me.'

"Matthew closes his gospel with the Great Commission (Matthew 28:16-20). As he ascended into heaven, Jesus sent his apostles into the world to make disciples. I believe he continues to send us into the world to do the same thing."

The conclusion of Matthew's story — the resurrection of Jesus and the Great Commission — shook the world's foundations. Nothing would ever be the same again for those who heard and believed the story. More importantly, Matthew's story has the power to shake our foundations *today*. I know. Matthew's story has shaken my foundations.

Once again, taking on the character of Matthew, Matt said, "It finally dawned on me. Jesus said it was going to happen, but none of us really believed it. How could we? No one had ever done this before. No one will ever do it again. He was dead, stone-cold dead. Now he is alive, never to die again. We saw the ultimate reversal. With our own eyes, we saw it."

Matt cleared his voice. He looked at Mary. Then he went on.

"As I said, 'It finally dawned on me.' I've been a member of this church all my life. I've heard the story of the resurrection every year. I thought I believed it, but it wasn't until I was preparing this presentation on Matthew that it really dawned on me that the story of Jesus' life, death, resurrection, and the Great Commission is aimed directly at me. I've been avoiding this for some years now, but I can avoid it no longer.

"I need your prayers for my future and our family's future. Yesterday, I quit my job as a tax collector at the Internal Revenue Service effective at the end of this month.

"Next month I will start pre-theological training in Greek, the language of the New Testament. God willing, in the fall I will begin my training at seminary to become a pastor."

The congregation was stunned.

Matt looked at Mary. She was smiling and crying. So was Matt's mother who was sitting next to Mary. Matt smiled back.

Questions For Your Personal Consideration And/Or Group Discussion

1. Re-read the quotes at the beginning of this section. What connection do you make between these quotes and the stories of Matthew and Matt?

2. What do you think about Matt's mother's comment: "You always have time for what you believe in"?

3. What is the difference between a tax collector in Jesus' time and one in our time?

4. What questions must have crossed Matthew's mind when Jesus said, "Follow me"?

5. How would you feel if you had been present at Matthew's house for the meal and party following Jesus' call to him?

6. How do the seven story principles in the Introduction to this book work in the stories of Matthew and Matt? List them here.
   a. Paradox
   b. Juxtaposition
   c. Space
   d. Overhearing
   e. Suspending the story
   f. Surprise
   g. Invitation

Chapter Nine

Thomas, The Doubter

John 20:19-31

It is not my purpose in this chapter to encourage doubt. It is my purpose to help the doubter know that he or she can be included in the fellowship of Christians. The resurrected Jesus said to Thomas, "Stop doubting and believe," but Jesus also said, "Put your finger here; see my hands. Reach out your hand and put it into my side." In other words, Jesus encouraged faith, not doubt, but he also included Thomas the doubter as one of his apostles. The story of Thomas is about the inclusiveness of a certain kind of doubt.

Sometimes we hear the problem put this way: "Either you believe or you don't believe." There is something to be said for this kind of either/or approach. This approach may help some people get off the fence and commit themselves to Jesus Christ as Lord and Savior. On the other hand, some people are offended by the simple either/or approach. In their view, belief is complex, not simple. They want to be included, yet they have some doubts that just won't go away. That's where the story of Thomas, the doubter, can help.

The Story Of Thomas
First let's look at the story of Thomas as we know it from the New Testament. Then we'll look at Thomas, the doubter.

The story of Thomas may be divided into seven parts:

1. his call,
2. his devotion,
3. his confusion,
4. his doubts,
5. his reversal and confession,
6. his renewal, and
7. his missionary life.

First, Thomas was called by Jesus to be one of the twelve apostles (Matthew 10:3). His other name is *Didymus*, a Greek name, meaning "the twin." We don't know who his twin brother (or sister) is. We do know that in all of our hearts and minds there are twins called faith and doubt.

Second, in John 11:7-8 we read of Thomas' devotion to Jesus. The other apostles were astonished that Jesus intended to go back to Judea where there would be certain conflict and possibly death. They said, "Rabbi, a short while ago the Jews tried to stone you, and yet you are going back there?" Determined to share the peril, Thomas said to the rest of the disciples, "Let us also go, that we may die with him" (John 11:16).

Thomas' doubt is well known. His devotion is often neglected. He was willing to go with Jesus back to where Lazarus had just died, even if it meant death. He urged the others to do the same. The paradoxical nature of Thomas, the doubter, and Thomas, the devoted disciple, is an encouragement to everyone who is torn between these two poles. The juxtaposition between these two personality characteristics is not limited to Thomas. Like a Bach cantata, we hear a point and counterpoint flowing back and forth in Thomas.

Third, Thomas, like the other apostles, was often confused by what Jesus said. When confused, he openly said so, at least he did so when Jesus talked about where he was going next. In John 14:6, Jesus said that he was going to prepare a place for his followers. He added that they knew where he was going. Thomas responded,

"Lord, we don't know where you are going, so how can we know the way?" Jesus suspended the question and added tension by raising the question to a higher level. He stunned Thomas and the others by replying, "I am the way, the truth and the life. No one comes to the Father except through me" (John 14:6). In this passage, we hear an invitation for people to follow this way, which Jesus calls elsewhere, "the narrow gate and the road less traveled" (paraphrase of Matthew 7:13-14).

Fourth, Thomas showed the doubting side of his nature when the other apostles reported that they had seen the resurrected Lord when Thomas was not present (John 20:19-31). We don't know why Thomas was not present in the upper room that first Easter evening, only that he wasn't there. Perhaps he was so gripped with grief at Jesus' death that he insisted on being alone. When the others told him that they had seen Jesus alive again, he refused to believe it. "Unless I see the nail marks in his hands and put my finger where the nails were, and put my hand into his side, I will not believe it," he said (John 20:25b). He refused to take someone else's word for a thing like that.

A week later, Thomas was in the upper room when the resurrected Jesus made another appearance. "Peace be with you," the Lord said. Then he addressed Thomas directly. "Put your finger here; see my hands. Reach out your hand and put it into my side. Stop doubting and believe." Much has been made about the "stop doubting" portion of Jesus' statement. Not enough has been said about Jesus' invitation to Thomas to do what he said he must do in order to believe. That means that Jesus took Thomas' doubts seriously. As in so many cases in his ministry, Jesus started with Thomas where he was. Then he raised him to a higher level of devotion. Note that Thomas never did what he said he had to do to believe. Instead he fell at Jesus' feet.

Fifth, Thomas' confession is an amazing reversal. It is a long way from Thomas' "I'm from Missouri and you've got to show me" attitude to an act of prostration at the feet of Jesus. It is one of the quickest and most unexpected personal turning points in human history. The words of Thomas' reversal are stunning. "My Lord and my God."

Sixth, Thomas, along with the other apostles, experienced renewal when Jesus met them while casting their nets on the Sea of Galilee (John 21:1-8). They were renewed again after the ascension in the upper room in a powerful prayer meeting (Acts 1:12-14). The spiritual renewal they experienced was for the missionary work they had before them to spread the gospel to all nations.

Seventh, Thomas, like the others, went into the world with the good news of Jesus' life, death, and resurrection. According to tradition, Thomas was a missionary in Parthia and Persia (today's Iran) and later brought the gospel to India. In India, the devoted apostle suffered martyrdom in Madras (at a place today called "Thomas' Mount").

Thomas, The Doubter

The story of Thomas, the devoted doubter, is an encouragement to folks who struggle with their faith. Jesus included Thomas, in spite of his doubts. Doubters and skeptics today can be included, too. What if E. S. Martin is right in suggesting that even in the most fervent believer, there are lingering doubts?

> *Within my earthly temple there's a crowd,*
> *There's one of us that's humble, one that's proud.*
> *There's one broken-hearted for his sins,*
> *There's one that unrepentant sits and grins;*
> *There's one that loves his neighbor as himself,*
> *And one that cares for naught but fame and self.*
> *From much corroding care I should be free,*
> *If I could once determine which is me.*[7]

Actually, both are me. As Luther put it, Christians are simultaneously saints and sinners. Faith and doubt are often found in the same person. Some Christians doubt more; some less. Since the origin of most doubts is our pain, we need to doubt our doubts and focus on our faith. The father of the epileptic boy shows us the way of overcoming doubt by confessing the need for help with unbelief. When we see doubt as a problem to be overcome, and ask for help by increased faith, we are on the way to spiritual health.

The father of an epileptic boy said it best. He had just said to Jesus, "If you are able to do anything (to help my boy), have pity on us and help us." Jesus replied, "If you are able? All things can be done for one who believes." The father of the epileptic boy replied, "I believe; help my unbelief" (Mark 9:24 NRSV).

In other words, we have both belief and unbelief in our hearts. We need help with the unbelief. When we give our attention to our belief and seek help for our unbelief, we are on the journey called faith. E. Stanley Jones put it this way, "What gets your attention gets you."

If we give our attention to our doubts, and only glance at our faith, our doubts will get us. On the other hand, if we give our attention to our faith and only glance at our doubts, our faith will get us. In the story of Thomas, we see how the apostle almost fell off the cliff called skepticism, but was able to refocus his attention on the Lord when the resurrected Jesus met him in the upper room and invited him to do the very thing he said he must do if he was to believe, namely touch the risen Lord. The touch never took place. The refocused Thomas looked at Jesus' wounded hands and fell at Jesus' wounded feet and said, "My Lord and my God."

Everything Changed When Thomas Focused On Jesus' Wounds

In my experience, most doubters raise questions because of their own wounds. Most doubts are not purely intellectual reservations. Many doubts come from hurting situations, sicknesses of body or mind, unresolved conflicts, and intolerable situations. In other words, when we are wounded, we tend to blame someone else. Often, we blame God for what seems out of control. In terms of what E. Stanley Jones said, our wounds get our attention. When our wounds get our attention, we sometimes turn away from the only one who can help us with our wounds. Most doubts are not resolved by intellectual exercises, rational conclusions, or philosophical propositions. Most doubts are resolved by looking at the wounds of Jesus, the wounded healer.

That's what Thomas did. He took his eyes off his disappointment in how things turned out and his own severe loneliness at the

113

loss of his Lord and looked at the wounds of Jesus. Jesus, the wounded healer, helps us to see our doubts from the perspective of his vicarious death. When we look at Jesus' suffering and death, we can find a passage through what seemed like dark, shadowy valleys of hopelessness. As Psalm 23 says, "Even though I walk through the valley of the shadow of death, I will fear no evil, for you are with me; your rod and your staff, they comfort me."

Jesus resolves pain and suffering not by removing it, but by walking right into it and taking the burdens of each of us upon himself. Sometimes the only way out is through.

A little girl was looking at the picture of the resurrected Jesus one day. The children around her were singing and dancing. She was just staring at the wounds in Jesus' feet and hands. Her teacher asked her what she was thinking.

"I wonder if it hurt," she said.

Yes, little girl, it hurt for Jesus to be crucified for us. "He was wounded for our transgressions." It hurt more than we will ever know. He took all our sins, our pains, our suffering, and our burdens upon himself at one point in time and died for us. That's what Thomas saw in the wounds of Christ. He saw what Jesus had gone through to make it possible for him to believe.

Thomas is called the Twin for a good reason. He may have physically been a twin, but in addition he struggled between the pull of the inner twins in his heart. When wounded, Thomas felt like we feel when things go wrong. "Where is God now when I need him the most?" Then he was invited to look away from his own wounds to the wounds of the wounded healer. Everything looks different when we focus on what has been done for us by Jesus' vicarious death and resurrection. That focus makes possible the ultimate turn around from self to God.

When in pain, the psalmists doubted God big time, but came back from their state of near despair when they refocused on the Lord. Read Psalm 73 and feel the wounds of the ancient poet who suffered untold burdens because the unrighteous prospered while the faithful suffered. The psalmist went into the place of worship and got the big picture that all of us will have to face God on the day of judgment. Then he could say, "Nevertheless I am continually with thee" (Psalm 73:23 RSV).

Martin Luther experienced *anfectungen*, a soul despair beyond description. He thought, "I am a sinner. God hates sin. There's no hope." Then he looked at Jesus who clothes the unworthy sinner in righteousness. That look at Jesus' wounds changed his perspective. He saw that we have "alien righteousness," righteousness that is given freely, not earned. That's why Luther was such a man of faith. He was not a man of faith because he had no doubts or wounds, but precisely because, like Thomas, he saw his wounds in the light of Jesus' wounds.

That's what the psalmist meant. That's what Thomas expressed. That's why Thomas' confession rings true today. As to his own strength, it was washed away before he said, "My Lord and my God."

What some churches and pulpit-pounders have advocated is a watered-down faith that suggests that doubt is wrong and that a Christian is a mild-mannered, pious-sounding, ever-smiling, happy, cheerful, and totally unrealistic dud. That kind of superficial faith doesn't have enough power to help us punch our way out of a paper bag. The biblical corrective is the counterpoint of doubt and faith, a dynamic faith that has struggled with wounds and found resolution in the wounds of Jesus, the wounded healer.

A poet put it this way: "Doubt is pain too lonely to know that faith is his twin brother." Thomas struggled with the twin voices of doubt and faith. When he met Jesus, his doubts didn't just automatically go away. They went to a deeper level. At the deepest level, as he approached despair at the loss of his Lord, Jesus appeared and showed him his wounds. "Look, Thomas. See, Thomas. Feel, Thomas. It's me."

Some people doubt little; some more. When wounded, most of us doubt God at the very time we need to see what he has done for us in the suffering, death, and resurrection of Jesus.

At these times, take another look at the wounds of Jesus and say with Thomas, "My Lord and my God." That's what the story

115

of Thomas is all about. In the upper room, Thomas met Jesus again, but it was as if for the first time he saw him for what he is, the wounded healer.

Questions For Your Personal Consideration
And/Or Group Discussion

1. How does the story of Thomas intersect with your story?

2. What reversals have you experienced in life?

3. How is the story of Thomas an invitation for people to meet Jesus today?

4. Do you agree or disagree with E. S. Martin's poem about the crowd in our "temples"?

5. Do you agree or disagree with the statement: "If we give our attention to our doubts and only glance at our faith, our doubts will get us"?

6. Do you agree with the statement: "Sometimes the only way out is through"?

7. One man described the struggle within our hearts as a fight between two dogs. "Which dog wins?" someone asked him. "The one I feed," he said. Do you agree or disagree?

Part Four

Post-Resurrection

Vision

Some people do not see.
  This is called blindness.
Some people see, but do not understand.
  This is called sight.
Some people see beyond what they behold.
  This is called vision.

— Anonymous

Where there is no vision, the people perish....

— Proverbs 29:18 (KJV)

In a loud voice they sang:
"Worthy is the Lamb, who was slain,
to receive power and wealth and wisdom and strength
and honor and glory and praise!"

— Revelation 5:12

Chapter Ten

John, The Visionary

John 8:21

His name was John. Zebedee and Salome were his parents. His older brother was James. Jesus called these two brothers "sons of thunder," apparently because they had "short fuses" and often "shot off at the mouth" without thinking much about what they said. In that respect, James and John were like Peter, their partner in the fishing business on the Sea of Galilee. One day Jesus came to their fishing boat and called them to follow him. They accepted the invitation, despite the hardship of leaving their home, their family, and their business. John was a hot-headed fisherman. He became John the visionary apostle. Quite a reversal.

The change was not easy. When resistance came to Jesus and his followers in a certain Samaritan village, James and John said that Jesus should call down fire from the heavens and destroy the village. The look on Jesus' face told them that their anger and quick judgment were out of place in the new life to which he had called them. That same look on Jesus' face froze the brothers in place the day their mother asked him for places of honor in his kingdom for her sons. Jesus told them he came to serve, not to be served. He didn't seek honor. He didn't want his followers to seek it. It was a slow learning process for young John to become a man filled with wisdom and vision.

At the cross, Jesus told his mother, Mary, that John was to be her new son. He told John to take care of his new mother, Mary.

119

That, too, was part of the learning process of maturity. Caring for another person is a way in which we can grow beyond our self-centeredness. John learned. After the resurrection, John, like the other apostles, became a missionary for Christ.

By the time he wrote the gospel that bears his name, John was an old man. He had grown into a wise and visionary man of God. He wanted to do more than just tell the story of what happened to Jesus. He wanted the meaning to come through to his readers.

When John wrote his gospel, three other gospels were in circulation: Matthew, Mark, and Luke. Therefore, John did not tell the details of Jesus' birth and life like the other writers. Instead, he spoke with vision of the meaning of those events in terms of light and life for the world. About Jesus' birth, John writes:

> *In the beginning was the Word, and the Word was with God, and the Word was God. He was with God in the beginning. Through him all things were made; without him nothing was made that has been made. In him was life, and that life was the light of men. The light shines in the darkness, but the darkness has not understood it.*
> — John 1:1-5

John had the vision. Jesus was divine. He was God incarnate. He was also a man, God who put on flesh and dwelt among us full of grace and truth. Those who believed saw the glory that John saw in Christ. Vision means seeing light beyond the darkness of people's rejection of the truth. Jesus was more than a good man. He was more than a great teacher. He was beyond the boundaries of a wonderful example. Jesus was the Word made flesh. John saw it.

John's vision in writing the story of Jesus was to help people see the glory of God in Jesus and to be transferred from the kingdom of darkness to the kingdom of light. The first sign of this change from darkness to light in the Gospel of John is the wedding of Cana where Jesus turned ordinary water into extraordinary wine. Ordinary people were to become extraordinary by their faith in Christ. They were given life and light.

120

John saw Jesus' vision for Nicodemus, that he would become a new man in Christ. At the time, Nicodemus didn't see it. John reports the words of Jesus: "I tell you the truth, no one can enter the kingdom of God unless he is born of water and the Spirit. Flesh gives birth to flesh, but the Spirit gives birth to spirit" (John 3:5). John also reports that Nicodemus was the first man to hear those incomparable words about God's intentions for all his people to come into eternal life and light.

For God so loved the world that he gave his one and only Son, that whoever believes in him shall not perish but have eternal life. For God did not send his Son into the world to condemn the world, but to save the world through him. — John 3:16-17

Eternal life and light were also offered to the Samaritan woman at the well. John 4:1-42 records the invitation of Jesus to the woman and the Samaritans of her town. Samaria stood between the northern kingdom of Israel and the southern kingdom of Judah. In a journey from one kingdom to the other, righteous Jews of the time walked around Samaria, avoiding contamination from the hated Samaritans. Samaritans were hated because they had compromised Jewish monotheism and morality during the captivity of the Jews in Babylon (today's Iraq) beginning in 586 B.C. When the Jews returned from the Babylonian captivity, they found that the Samaritans had intermarried with pagans and practiced idolatry.

The apostles, including John, were Jewish. They must have wondered why Jesus insisted on going into Samaria. They were shocked further when they returned from securing food and found Jesus talking to a Samaritan woman. In Jesus' day, women were forbidden to talk about God and religion. Women were considered more like property than people. Jesus was talking to and listening to a Samaritan woman at the well. The incongruity in the story jumps out at us.

The woman dashed off toward town, telling everyone, "Come, see a man who told me everything I ever did. Could this be the Christ?" Eternal life and the light of Christ were beginning to dawn on her. She was beginning to get a new vision for what her life could be. The townspeople caught that vision, too. John 4:39 reports, "Many of the Samaritans from that town believed in him because of the woman's testimony." But after listening to the Lord for two days, they saw for themselves the vision of the new life in Christ. "They said to the woman, 'We no longer believe just because of what you said; now we have heard for ourselves, and we know that this man really is the Savior of the world' " (John 4:42). There was a great reversal in their lives as they came to trust in Jesus Christ. It is paradoxical that in the Gospel of John, the hated Samaritans became some of the first followers of Christ.

Story after story in the Gospel of John shows how Jesus brought the vision of new life and light to all kinds of people. That new vision for life is demonstrated in the healing of the lame man (John 5:1-15), the healing of the blind man (John 9:1-12), and the forgiveness offered to the woman caught in adultery (John 8:3-11).

The "I AM" sayings in the Gospel of John show us new dimensions of the eternal life and light Jesus offered people. Jesus said:

- "I am the bread of life" (John 6:35).
- "I am the light of the world" (John 8:12 and John 9:1-5).
- "Before Abraham was, I am" (John 8:58).
- "I am the gate for the sheep." (John 10:7).
- "I am the good shepherd" (John 10:11).
- "I am the resurrection and the life" (John 11:25).
- "I am the true vine" (John 15:1).

"I AM" is the name God gave to himself in the encounter with Moses in Exodus 3:13-15. Jesus used that name for himself. Jesus was claiming divinity. He was either an egocentric maniac or what he claimed to be — the Messiah who was God incarnate who was bringing a new vision of eternal life and light to people.

In the Gospel of John, we must wrestle with John's vision of Jesus offering eternal life and light, not only in the future, but in the present as well. Jesus says, "I tell you the truth, whoever hears my word and believes him who sent me *has* eternal life" (John

5:24). That's present-tense religion. Eternal life isn't complete until the hereafter, but it begins in the here and now. The Apostle John shows that people's lives change when they are confronted by the Lord Jesus Christ. People in John's Gospel and people today are given vision by Christ to see beyond the materialistic world.

In 1960, Mary Swanson heard a sermon on Saint John's concept of eternal life and light. It changed her life. The text was, "I am the light of the world" (John 8:12). The pastor wasn't an eloquent preacher, but his sincerity and integrity were known by all his people. He lifted Christ high before the minds of the parishioners that day. He used passages from John's Gospel to show: Jesus as the one in whom there is life and light (1:4); Jesus as the true light that enlightens every man (1:9); Jesus who brings light to the world (3:19 and 12:46); and Jesus, the Great I AM, who brings light to all (8:12).

Mary was deeply moved by the words. She was a nurse at Augustana Hospital. She had been thinking about mission work for some time. That sermon confirmed her call. She contacted the board of world missions. After ten months of waiting and special training, Mary was sent to Africa to bring the vision of Christ as the light of the world to the people there. Again and again she read the Gospel of John. She shared the story of the visionary gospel with all the people she met.

When Mary returned for furlough from time to time, she saw the contrast between the vital, new converts she saw in Tanzania and many church members who seemed to be little more than cultural Christians. "Many seem to take faith for granted," she told her pastor. Her pastor agreed and added sadly, "It is really hard to interest people in world mission work today. They seem preoccupied with themselves."

On the thirtieth anniversary of her call to missionary work, Mary was back in America on furlough, teaching in as many churches as possible, trying to open the eyes of as many people as possible. Normally a very energetic person, Mary found that she was getting very tired as she traveled around America. She saw a doctor who told her, "There is a problem with your heart. You

123

need by-pass surgery. You should give up your mission work and stay in America."

She thought about the advice of the doctor as she continued her teaching ministry in the churches of America. She went to a large department store to buy a globe to help her in her teaching ministry. She spotted one that she especially liked. What she didn't like was the price. On a missionary's salary, it would take some serious stretching to buy it. She asked the salesman about it. "This one costs more," he said, "because it is lighted from the inside." Smiling, he added, "A lighted world costs more."

"Yes," Mary replied, "I know." She bought the expensive globe and used it in her presentations.

She had the heart surgery prescribed by the doctor. After a period of recovery, the doctor said, "You'll be fine as long as you don't go back to Africa and the stress of mission work there." Shortly thereafter, Mary talked to her pastor and made a decision.

Mary returned to Tanzania where, after a year of intense work as a medical missionary, she died of a heart attack.

At Mary's funeral, her pastor preached on John 8:12, the words of Jesus: "I am the light of the world." His sermon title was "A Lighted World Costs More."

That's what the Gospel of John is all about.

Questions For Your Personal Consideration And/Or Group Discussion

1. John was the youngest of the apostles, yet Jesus chose him, along with Peter and James, to be a part of his "inner circle." Based on what you know about John why do you think Jesus included John?

2. John called himself "the one who Jesus loved" (John 13:23). From the cross, Jesus appointed John to care for his mother. What do you think this means?

3. In John 12:32, we read Jesus' words, "... and I, when I am lifted up from the earth will draw all men to myself." What do you think this means?

4. Read John 15:1-8. What does it mean that Jesus is the vine and we are the branches?

5. In what ways do the stories of Mary Swanson and the Apostle John intersect?

6. Read John 21:1-25. What does this passage mean?

Tips For Teachers, Pastors, And Group Leaders

1. This book may be used for adult education classes and small groups. It may also be used with teenagers in classes and groups.

2. The questions at the end of each chapter can be used to start discussions.

3. Remember, you are a leader, not a lecturer. Your job is to try to get people in your group involved in the discussion.

4. Breaking into small groups of two for discussion of questions and reporting back to the whole group is one way to assure the participation of all group members.

5. Recommended books by Ron Lavin with questions at the end of each chapter for group discussion:
    *   *Way To Grow!* (Dynamic Church Growth Through Small Groups) — provides models and topics for small group discussion.
    *   *I Believe; Help My Unbelief* (Another Look At The Apostles' Creed)
    *   *Stories To Remember* (Another Look At The Parables Of Jesus)
    *   *Abba* (Another Look At The Lord's Prayer)
    *   *Saving Grace* (Another Look At The Word And Sacraments)
    *   *The Big Ten* (Another Look At The Ten Commandments)
    *   *Turning Griping Into Gratitude* (A Study In The Psalms)

6. These books are all available from CSS Publishing Company, 517 South Main Street, Lima, Ohio, 45804. Phone orders: 800-537-1030; Fax: 1-419-228-9184; web address: csspub.com. Each participant should have a copy of this book. To order books for your group, have CSS bill your church or you personally. Distribute the books and collect the money from the participants.

Endnotes

Introduction — Section One
1. David Rhoads and Donald Michie, *Mark As Story* (Philadelphia: Fortress Press, 1982), p. 129.

2. Fulton Oursler, *The Greatest Story Ever Told* (Garden City: New Jersey: Doubleday and Co., Inc., 1949).

Introduction — Section Two
3. Ron Lavin, *Stories To Remember* (Lima, Ohio: CSS Publishing Co., 2002).

Chapter Two
4. John V. Taylor, The Go Between God (Philadelphia: Fortress, 1972), p. 93.

Chapter Four
5. For more information on the "I AM" sayings of Jesus, see Ron Lavin's *The Great I AM* (Lima, Ohio: CSS Publishing Co., 1995).

6. For more information about biblical paradoxes, see Ron Lavin's I *Believe, Help My Unbelief* (Lima, Ohio: CSS Publishing Co., 2001).

Chapter Nine

7. E. S. Martin, as quoted by Melvin A Hammerberg in *My Body Broken* (Philadelphia: Fortress, 1963), p. 15.